35 Guided Meditation Scripts Volume 1

Visualization, imagery, body scan, body awareness, breath control and awareness, and relaxation techniques for self-healing, peace, calm, anxiety, and overcoming challenges

By Rayna Zara

Dedication

This book is dedicated to my son, Leo, for all the vibrancy and joy you bring into my life and for inspiring me to do better and be better at life.

Introduction

This book contains 35 guided meditation scripts. The various meditation scripts incorporate techniques such as visualizations and imagery, breathing exercises, breathe awareness, body scans, and mindful exercises. The meditations range from 5 minutes up to 1 hour. There is something for both beginners and novice meditators.

How to Use this book.
The Meditation scripts herein are ideal for use by yoga teachers, psychologists, counselors, meditation teachers, hypnotherapists or individuals. You can read them to your students/clients or record for personal or professional use but not for commercial use.

Each meditation has an indication for when you should be silent and for how long. Pace yourself as you read to ensure that your tone and speed give the audience a calming experience.

Table of Contents

Chapter 1: Breath Meditation

This section contains various breath-focused meditations that incorporate different breathing techniques such as breath control, deep breathing and breath observance to cultivate calm and relieve stress.

These are ideal for use as a simple calming and grounding practice at the beginning of a counselling session, at the beginning or end of a yoga class, or as brief breaks in workshops, seminars or conferences. Individuals can use these breathing meditations for quick relaxation and as tools for concentration and focus.

These meditations are ideal for use as a simple calming and grounding practice at the beginning of a counselling session, at the beginning or end of a yoga class, or as brief breaks in workshops, seminars or conferences.

1. Breath Meditation 1 (Technique: Breath Control)

Find a comfortable and quiet place for your meditation

You may either sit on the ground with your legs crossed or on a chair with feet on the floor.

Take a deep breath in and as you exhale gently close your eyes.

Take another deep breath in and lift your shoulders towards your ears - contracting the muscles around your neck and your shoulders.

Now, exhale, and gently drop your shoulders away from your ears allowing any tension around your chest, shoulders and neck to melt away.

Become aware of the contact between your buttocks and the chair or the ground. Surrender the weight of your body to the surface beneath you.

Lengthen your spine so that you assume an upright and alert posture.

Inhale through your nose, completely fill up your lungs and exhale through your mouth, completely empty out your lungs.

Once again inhale through your nose, and exhale through your mouth.

Keep breathing in through the nose and out through the mouth.

(1 minute)

With every inhale completely fill up the lungs and with every exhale completely empty out. Keep breathing deeply in and out

(1 minute)

Take one more deep breath in and exhale completely. Gently open your eyes and get on with the rest of your day.

May you be happy, may you be peaceful, may you be harmonious.

Love and light to you.

2. Breath Meditation 2 (Technique: Breath Control)

Find a comfortable and quiet place for your meditation. You may either sit on the ground with your legs crossed or on a chair with feet on the floor.

Take a deep breath in and as you exhale gently close your eyes.

Take another deep breath in and lift your shoulders towards your ears - contracting the muscles around your neck and your shoulders.

Now, exhale, and gently drop your shoulders away from your ears allowing any tension around your chest, shoulders and neck to melt away.

Become aware of the contact between your buttocks and the chair or the ground. Surrender the weight of your body on the surface beneath you.

Lengthen your spine so that you assume an upright and alert posture. Inhale through your nose, completely filling up your lungs and exhale through your mouth, completely emptying out the lungs.

Once again inhale through your nose, and exhale through your mouth. Keep breathing in through the nose and out through the mouth.

(1 minute)

With every inhale completely fill up the lungs and with every exhale completely empty out. Keep breathing deeply in and out

(1 minute)

Now, breath in and at the end of the inhale hold your breath in for account of 3, Part your lips slightly and gently release the air out through your mouth. At the end of the exhale, hold your breath out for a count of 3.

Close your mouth and breath in again, as you complete the inhale hold your breath in for 3 counts Slightly open your mouth to exhale and again hold the exhale out for 3 counts.

Stay alert and aware as you repeat this technique a few more times

(2 minutes)

Now resume normal breathing. In and out through your nose.

(30 seconds)

Notice how your mind and body feel. Notice any sounds or smells around you. Gently open your eyes. Take a few moments of silence before getting on with the rest of your day.

May you be happy,

may you be peaceful,

may you be harmonious.

Love and light to you

3. Breath Meditation 3 (Technique: Breath Control)

Find a comfortable and quiet place for your meditation.

Either sit on the ground with legs crossed or a chair with feet on the floor.
Take a deep breath in and as you exhale place your hands on your chest – one on top of the other.

Inhale deeply and notice your chest rise. Exhale completely and notice your chest fall.
Once again inhale, notice the rising of the chest.
Exhale, notice your chest fall.

Keep breathing deeply as you pay attention to the sequential rise and fall of your chest.

(1 Minute)

When your mind wanders, bring back your attention to your breathing and your chest. Do not beat yourself about it.

(1 minute)

Take one more deep breath in and as you exhale gently bring your hands down to rest your palms on your thighs.

Come back to your normal breathing. Pay attention to your nostril and notice your breath as it comes in and goes out.

(1.30 minutes)

Notice how your body and mind feel. Feel your feet on the ground.
Pay attention to what is happening in your room and outside in the near vicinity.
Set an intention to bring the sense of calm you feel to the rest of your day.

May you be happy,
may you be peaceful,
may you be harmonious.
Love and light to you

4. Breath Meditation 4 (Technique: Breath Control)

In this meditation, you will practice a breathing technique whereby you will count to five on the inhale and then to 8 on the exhale. Holding the exhale longer activates the parasympathetic nervous system which encourages the body to relax. The mind also transitions from the beta state to an alpha state where fewer neurons are firing. This further promotes relaxation. Needless to say, you are also able to focus and concentrate better in the alpha state.

This guided meditation is suitable for both beginners and ~~novice~~ regular meditators. You can do it first thing in the morning or any time during the day when you feel stressed out, anxious or you simply need a break from your day. It also helps to reduce fear. Therefore, you can do it ahead of a stressful meeting or interview or a ~~scary~~ doctor's/dentist appt. appointment.

Physiologically, this technique also increases your lung capacity and promotes better oxygen circulation within the body. In case you become dizzy when doing it, reduce you counts to 2-3 for inhales and 3-5 for exhales. You can do this meditation either seated or lying down. Throughout the session there will be moments of silence for you to breathe.
Assume your preferred meditation posture and close your eyes.
Take a deep breath in and exhale through your mouth.
Take 3 more deep breaths through your nose.

15 seconds

Assume your natural breathing in and out through your nose.

30 seconds

Notice how you feel emotionally, mentally and physically. Just being aware of your body as it is in the present moment.

30 seconds

Now, inhale deeply to a count of 5.
Open your lips slightly and exhale slowly to a count of 8.
Close your mouth at the end of the exhale.

Again, breath in deeply through your nose for a count of 5 and exhale slowly through your mouth for a count of 8.

Continue practicing this breathing technique. Inhale through your nose for 5 counts and exhale through your mouth for 8 counts

15 seconds

You may reduce or increase the number of counts to suit your lung capacity. The idea is to have 2-3 counts difference between the inhale and the exhale.
90 seconds

Continue practicing this breathing technique. Inhale through your nose for 5 counts and exhale through your mouth for 8 counts

2 minutes

Now, take an equal inhale and an equal exhale.
Bring your attention back to the rest of your body
Then to your surroundings.

When you are ready, gently open your eyes and get on
with the rest of your day.

5. Breath Meditation 5 (Technique: Breath Control)

Assume your preferred meditation posture (either seated or lying down) and close your eyes.
Take a deep breath in and exhale through your mouth.
Take 3 more deep breaths through your nose.

15 seconds

Assume your natural breathing in and out through your nose.

30 seconds

Notice how you feel emotionally, mentally and physically. Just being aware of your body as it is in the present moment.

30 seconds

Now, inhale deeply to a count of 5.
Open your lips slightly and exhale slowly to a count of 8.
Close your mouth at the end of the exhale.

Again, breath in deeply through your nose for a count of 5 and exhale slowly through your mouth for a count of 8.

Continue practicing this breathing technique. Inhale through your nose for 5 counts and exhale through your mouth for 8 counts

15 seconds

You may reduce or increase the number of counts to suit your lung capacity. The idea is to have 2-3 counts difference between the inhale and the exhale.
90 seconds

Continue practicing this breathing technique. Inhale through your nose for 5 counts and exhale through your mouth for 8 counts

2 minutes

Now, take an equal inhale and an an equal exhale.
Bring your attention back to the rest of your body
Then to your surroundings.

When you are ready, gently open your eyes and get on with the rest of your day.

6. Breath Meditation 6 (Technique: Breath Awareness)

Find a comfortable and quiet place for your meditation. Either sit on the ground with legs crossed or on a chair with feet on the floor.

Take a deep inhale and as you exhale gently close your eyes.

Adjust your body as need be to find a comfortable position.

Take another deep breath in, hold the breath in, and slowly exhale completely emptying your lungs.

Now, assume your normal natural breathing. Let go any deliberate control on your breath.

(1minute)

Your breathing might be shallow or deep. Maybe there is a pause between the inhale and the exhale, or between the exhale and the inhale.

Maybe there is no pause. Just notice your breathing as it is.

(1 minute)

Bring your attention to your nostrils. Inside the nostrils and on the rings of the outer edge of the nostril. Notice if you can feel a brush of the air as it goes in and out. Is the air warm or is it cold?

(45 seconds)

Do you notice any sensations around the nostrils?

Maybe contraction and expansion, some heat or cold, maybe a tingling sensation or there might be no sensations at all.
With an alert mind, remain aware of each inhale and each exhale as you survey what is happening around your nostril.

(1minute)

When your mind wanders, notice it and bring back your attention to the nostrils.

(2 minutes)

Take a deep breath in and exhale with a sigh.

Gently open your eyes, notice your surroundings and move on with the rest of your day.

May you be happy, may you be peaceful, may you be harmonious.
Love and light to you

7. Breath Meditation 7 (Technique: Breath Awareness)

Start in a comfortable sitting position.

Spine lengthened, torso upright and shoulders dropping away from your ears.

Take a deep breath in, hold your breath in and exhale out, empty your lungs completely.

(10 seconds)

Take another deep breath in, hold, and exhale, hold your breath out for four, three, two and one.

Now, resume your normal natural breath. In and out through your nose. Let your breathing assume a natural rhythm.
 Do not deliberately make it shallower or deeper.

(15 seconds)

Notice the parts of your body where you breathing manifests.

(15 seconds)

Notice the part of your body where your breathing manifests most conspicuously. It could be the rise and fall of your belly, or the rise and fall of your chest or a strong sensation on your nostrils and inhale and exhale.

(30 seconds)

Now, take your attention to your chest. Keep your awareness on your chest and observe how a complete breath cycle manifests in your chest.

(20 seconds)

Is the rise on the inhale longer than the fall on the exhale?

(20 seconds)

Is there a pause before the chest begins to fall on the exhale?

(20 seconds)

Is there a pause before the chest begins to rise on the next inhale?

(20 seconds)

Can you sense how shallow or deep your breathing is?

(20 seconds)

 Keep observing your breathing as it manifests on the chest area.

(1 minute)

Now take your attention to your nose.
Observe your breathing and how it manifests on your nostrils.

Stay with this awareness and observe a complete breath cycle.

(20 seconds)

How does the breathing pattern manifest here?

(15 seconds)

Is it shallow or deep?

(15 seconds)

Are there sensations arising on the nostrils as you inhale and exhale.

(10 seconds)

Is the air warm or cold?

(10 seconds)

Remain curious and alert of what is happening around your nose as you breath.

(30 seconds)

Now observe how a complete breath cycle manifests as air gets in through your nose, into the chest cavity and diaphragm and when the air is leaving the body from the diaphragm, the lungs and the nose.
Follow the air from your nose, to your chest and to your belly.

Then from your belly, to your chest and out through the nose.
Stay with each breath cycle.

(1 minute)

You will notice that your mental chatter will become quieter and majority of the thoughts will be in the background.
If your mind chatter becomes louder and you find yourself actively thinking, take a few deep breaths and resume observing your breath cycles.
One at a time.

(1 minute)

Notice how you feel.

(10 seconds)

Now, bring your attention back to your room.
Notice any sounds and noises within your vicinity. Become aware of what is happening around you in the present moment.

(10 seconds)

Take a deep breath in and a deep breath out.

Go on with the rest of your day and remember you can always come back to your breath whenever you need to feel more grounded and present.

May you be happy,

may you be peaceful,
may you be harmonious.

Love and light to you.

Chapter 2: Guided Visualizations and Imagery

Guided imagery and visualizations help you to totally relax
the body and mind. You can use them to relieve stress or
as a technique for self-hypnosis.

8. Guided Visualization 1 (for relaxation)

Lie on your back or sit upright in a comfortable position.

Inhale deeply and exhale deeply.

(5 seconds)

With every inhale imagine a relaxing wave of energy entering your body and with each exhale see the wave leave the body leaving you relaxed and calm.

(15 seconds)

Keep breathing in and out allowing the wave of energy to infiltrate every part of your body.

(30 seconds)

Now, imagine you are a taking a road trip to one of your favorite locations.

It is a warm sunny day.
The sky is clear and there is a gentle wind blowing your hair and cooling off your face with a fresh and soothing breeze.

(5 seconds)

The road is clear; you are enjoying the scenery as you listen to your favorite music.

(5 seconds)

You then notice a footpath a few meters away in the direction you are headed.
You are curious where the path is leading.
You get to the foot path and park the car beside it.
You peep through the window to see where the foot path leads.

(5 seconds)

In front of you is a path with a slight descend that is surrounded by grass that is about knee high.
You get out of the car and follow the footpath.
There is a gentle wind blowing the grass side to side. The tips of the grass gently touch your skin as you walk along the path.

(10 seconds)

A few meters down the foot path, you notice a river ahead of you.
You walk towards it.

(5 seconds)

The ground on the river bank is soft and moist.
The air around is crisp, clean and fresh.

(5 seconds)

You remove your shoes and step into the river.

(5 seconds)

The flowing water touches your skin with an equal firmness and gentleness.

(5 seconds)

You take a few steps into the waters towards a rock that is in the middle of the river.
You sit on the rock and extend your feet in the direction of the river is flowing towards.
You then close your eyes and listen around to the sound of the water as it flows and chirping of the birds that are nearby.

(15 seconds)

There is a gentle wind that is becoming stronger causing a rattling of the leaves on the nearby trees.
You stay here enjoying the sensation of the wind on skin and the water on your feet and shins.

(15 seconds)

You allow all the emotional weight you are carrying to be washed away and carried by the flowing water.

(15 seconds)

You stay here for a moment as you enjoy the connection you feel with nature and yourself.

(30 seconds)

When you are ready to leave, you take a deep breath in, stand up and begin to walk towards your car.

You carry the great view, the sense of connection and calmness with you on the rest of your trip and your life.

(1 minute)

Take a deep breath in, and bring your attention to your surroundings.
As you exhale, gently wiggle your fingers.
Slowly open your eyes and get on with the rest of your day.

May you be happy, may you be peaceful, may you be harmonious.
Love and light to you.

9. Guided Visualization 2 (for relaxation)

Let's get started

Find a comfortable seated position, in an upright posture.
Inhale deeply through your nose, part your lips slightly,
and exhale through your mouth.
Take 3 similar breaths.

30 seconds

With every inhale, imagine a cleansing breath sweeping
through your boy and as you exhale imagine all your
worries and fears leaving your body.

30 seconds

Now, close your mouth and take three deep breaths
through your nose.

30 seconds

Imagine a white light ray of light above the crown of your
head.
It is warm, energizing and calming.

Allow the white light to infiltrate your body from the
crown of your head, filling each cell on your head from the
crown, the entire skull, all the brain cells, and the face as it
washes away the low frequency energy of anxiety, worry
and fear held in your cells and fills them with calm, peace
and vibrancy.

15 seconds

Allow the light energy to linger around your head area as it thoroughly cleanses this part of the body of anxiety and fear.

30 seconds

Now, allow the light to flow to your arms, the biceps and triceps, the elbows and forearms, wrists, palms and all your fingers.
Let it wash away all the tension and anxiety held in this part of your body.

30 seconds

Let the light infiltrate your neck and the entire torso. It fills up your chest, respiratory organs and tissues, digestion system, cardiovascular system, renal system, the spine, all the back muscles and the belly.

10 seconds

As it infiltrates, it releases all the anxiety muscle memory held in your upper body.

15 seconds

Again, let the light and its energy linger here for a few more seconds.

30 seconds

Let the light enter your lower body.

From your pelvic area, down to the thighs, the knees, the legs, ankles, feet and toes.
It is cleaning up the anxious and worrisome energy in this part of the body.

20 seconds

Let it linger here for a few seconds.

30 seconds

Allow the light to leave your body and descend into the earth where the negative energy is dissolved.

10 seconds

A new white light emerges at the top of your head, infiltrates your entire body from the head to the feet filling you up with calm, peace and joy.
It lingers for a few more seconds to ensure no trace of fear and worry is left.

30seonds

Again, it leaves your body dissolves into the ground.
Notice how your body feels. Notice how your mind feels.

20 seconds

May you always know that this calm and peace is within reach.

10. Guided Visualization 3 (to get grounded)

Do you on some days feel insecure? Like, emotionally and physically you are out of balance. Yes, your feet are on the ground as you walk but energetically you are floating around aimlessly?

This guided meditation will help you to get centered and to feel sure within yourself, on such days. It is best to do it seated on a chair with both soles of the feet resting on the ground.

Let's begin

Sit up right on a chair or a stool with your spine and torso upright, shoulders relaxed and dropping downwards, neck tall, and head sturdy as if you are holding stack of books on top of your head.

Rest your palms facing down on your thighs, fingers slightly spread apart.
Rest your feet on the ground. Lift the ten toes off the ground and then rest them with ease back on the ground. Gently close your eyes.

Take a deep breath in and a deep breath out.
Another deep breath in, and a deep breath out.

Breath in, hold your breath in and exhale with a sigh through your mouth.

10 seconds

Assume your natural breathing, in and out through your nose.

45 seconds

Now, move your attention to your feet.
Notice the contact between your feet and the ground.

5 seconds

Imagine small strong roots growing from your feet into the ground.
The roots begin to grow deeper and wide into the earth.
Like the roots of a baobab tree that begin to emerge from a small seed and go forth to grow bigger and stronger as they penetrate deeply into the earth forming a strong foundation for a big baobab tree, so are the roots from your feet penetrating deep into the ground forming a firm foundation for you to stand on.

Like the roots of the baobab tree absorb water and nutrients from the soil and transport them to the trunk, leaves and branches for the tree to grow.
Visualize energy from the center of the earth flowing up the roots into your feel.

30 seconds

This energy flows upwards through your legs, into your thighs, upper body and head filling you up with all the good energy your need to survive, thrive and be healthy.

30 seconds

Your feet are firm on the ground and supported by the earth and your entire body is receiving all the energy it needs from the earth.

1 minute

Let your feet remain firm on the ground.

1 minute

Now, bring your attention back to your feet and your body.
Notice how you physically and energetically feel centered.
Take a deep breath in and a deep breath and out.
If you feel unbalanced within the course of the day, bring your attention to your feet on the ground and remember that the earth is supporting you.

11. Guided Visualization 4 (to let go worries and for deep relaxation)

This guided visualization is best for days when you have too much mental chatter or you are feeling worried it is holding you back from relaxing.

Lie down with feet extended in front of you, hands beside your body and palms facing up.
Adjust your body if need be until you find a comfortable position lying on your back. You may place a pillow underneath your knees.

Gently close your eyes and begin to take deep breaths.
In and out through your nose.

...1 minute...

Now, hold your breath for three counts between each inhale and exhale.

...1 minute...

Now, hold your breath for a count of four on the exhale.
Once again, breath in, hold your breath to a count of three and breath out, hold your breath to a count of four.

Keep doing this breathing technique.

...2 minutes...

Now assume your normal breathing. Unaltered. Natural.

...30 seconds...

Bring your attention to your nostril and observe the natural pattern of your breathe.

...2 minutes...

Imagine a reading table in the center of a dark room. Beside the table is one chair and on top of the table is a lamp shade at the middle.

On the table, there is a silver writing plate and a pen on top of it.

You walk towards the table, draw the chair backwards and seat down in front of the silver writing plate and the pen.

The entire room and table is dark apart from the center that is lit by the lampshade.
It is quiet.

You pick up the pen and begin to write all the thoughts in your minds.
First you begin with a recount of your day. Detailing everything: the good, the bad and those in between.

...30 seconds...

Detailing everything: the good, the bad and those in between.

...30 seconds...

You then begin to note down what you are grateful for.
People in your life,

...30 seconds...

things and situations,

...30 seconds...

as well as aspects of yourself you are grateful for.

...30 seconds...

Noting it all down.

...1 minute...

Now, you begin to write about all the heaviness you feel.
The worries
...30 seconds...

the fears,
...30 seconds...

about scary memories
...30 seconds...

and anxious thoughts of the future.
...30 seconds...

Mistakes you have made.
...30 seconds...

Hurtful things that others have done to you.
...30 seconds...

You write down the questions you are seeking answers for. Everything that is weighing you down and keeping you up and night.

You put it all down.
...1 minute...

When you finish, you place the pen back on the silver writing plate, lean back on the backrest of the chair, gently close your eyes and take a few deep breaths.

...30 seconds...

At the completion of your exhale, you get an urge to open your eyes. So, you gently open your eyes. In front of you the silver writing plate is shining. The light is manageable for your eyes so you look to investigate it.

You realize that the light is moving from one line to the other as it blends in and absorbs the writings.

The light moves from the top of the page, line by line, to the bottom of the page.

And as it moves you feel a sense of relief from all the things that have been weighing you down.

You get a sense that all will be fine and you will figure out what need to be figured out.
You let go and surrender wanting to control it all.

You also get a sense of deep gratitude for what is going on well in your life.
You feel a sense of joy, relaxation and calm.

You give yourself permission, permission to relax even if just for this moment.

...30 seconds...

With a gentle smile on your face, you pull back the chair, stand up and walk to your bed.
Here you lay down in your most comfortable sleeping position, bring the covers over your bed and let the weight of your body on the mattress.
A sense of stillness and calmness fills your body.

...30 seconds...

You are aware of the parts of the body in contact with each other, the beddings and the mattress.

...30 seconds...

Your feel relaxed.
You are aware of some body sensations here and there.
Some are obvious, others are subtle.

...30 seconds...

You don't feel the need to manipulate them. Only to be aware of them.
They are a reminder that your body is functioning and doing all it needs to, to keep you alive.

You notice your breathing, the rising and falling of your chest.

...30 seconds...

You notice the air come in and go out through your nose.

...30 seconds...

Your heart beating.
It is all effortless.

...30 seconds...

There is a relaxing sensation flowing from your toes to your head.
It permeates every part of your body cleansing all pent-up energy and tension.
It leaves you feeling calm and relaxed.
A subtle sensation flows from your head to toe.
You feel at home with your body.

...30 seconds...

Take a deep gentle breath. Wiggle your fingers and toes. When you are ready gently open your eyes.

12. Guided visualization 5 (Guided imagery for total body and mind relaxation).

Find a quiet place and assume a comfortable and alert posture.

(5 seconds)

bring your attention to your breathing. Take a deep breath in through your nose and observe as your stomach expands.

Hold it for a few seconds and exhale slowly through your mouth.

Once again breath in through your nose, hold your breath in and then breath out through your mouth.

Continue to breathe deeply, in and out through your nose.

(20 seconds)

Observe the movement of your stomach when you inhale and exhale. Notice how it expands and then contracts.

(20 seconds)

With each inhale allow your body to be washed with cleansing energy and with every exhale allow tension to leave your body.

(20 seconds)

Breath in as you say "I am relaxed", as you breath out say "I let go tension and stress".

(30 seconds

Breathe in

Breathe out

(30 seconds)

Now, bring your awareness to your feet.

Breathe in deeply fill your feet with cleansing energy, exhale slowly let your feet relax.

 (10 seconds)

Notice tension ease off from your feet.

Notice your toes relaxing.

(10 seconds)

Now, move your attention to your legs.

Envision a white light surrounding your legs and getting rid of all the tension there.

All the stiffness held in your shin evaporates in the air.

All the tension held in your calves diffuses in the air.

(10 seconds)

your legs feel heavy and relaxed.

(10 seconds)

Now, let your breath assume its normal rhythm.

(15 seconds)

Breathe in and envision a bright light moving to your upper legs.

Breathe out. Notice as it clears away all the tension.

Your thighs are now relaxed.

(20 seconds)

Become aware of your hips.

Breathe in

Envision a bright light surrounding your hips and bottom.

Visualize the bright light relaxing all the muscles in your hips and bottom.

As you breath out, visualize the light carrying away all the tightness and tension from your hips and bottom.

(20 seconds)

Take another deep breath.

Notice a bright light filling your spine.

Notice as your spine becomes bright and energetic.

As you exhale, visualize as the bright light release all the tension between the discs and the joints in your spine.

(20 seconds)

Notice how relaxed your body is becoming.

(20 seconds)

Take your awareness to your stomach.

Take a deep breath and observe as your stomach expands.

Breathe out slowly and observe the air carrying all the tension from your stomach.

(20 seconds)

Breathe in a beam of light.

Notice as it travels to your heart and chest.

Notice the light circling your heart in slow motion.

Become aware of your heart chakra opening.

Can you see the beautiful flower radiating a green light?

Feel all the tension in that area disappear, and your heart and chest relax as you exhale.

(30 seconds)

Take your awareness to your throat.

Take a deep breath.

Notice as the light enter through your nose to your throat.

Notice it getting rid of all the tension in your throat as you exhale.

(20 seconds)

Take a deep breath and release it slowly.

Become aware of your neck.

Notice all the tension lodged in your neck muscles.

Envision your neck moving in a circular motion.

Send the bright light to your neck and instruct it to clear all the tension in that area.

Breathe out all the stress and tension in your neck.

(20 seconds)

Breath in a beam of light.

Become aware of your face.

Notice all the tension in your eyes, nose, forehead, and jaw.

Notice as the light relaxes all your facial features.

Feel as your face become completely relaxed as you exhale.

(20 seconds)

Envision a green healing light on top of your head.

Notice as it circles your crown chakra.

Notice as the energy travels down to your body.

Feel it covering your entire head.

(10 seconds)

Notice it dropping through the veins in your neck.

Feel it dropping further to your shoulders.

(10 seconds)

Observe as the green light fills your left and right hand.

As it drops down to your body, it becomes stronger.

Notice as it fills your heart.

Notice how relaxed your chest is

(20 seconds)

Your heart expands with love and compassion.

(10 seconds)

Notice the green light dropping to your stomach and unravelling any tension left there.

It also flows down your entire back.

Feel it traveling between the veins and the muscles in your back.

Feel the green light strengthening your spine.

(20 seconds)

Now, notice as it circles your hips and bottom.

Feel it tightening and releasing the muscles in your bottom and hips.

Notice as it relaxes your hips and bottom.

(10 seconds)

Visualize the green light separating to form two streams.

Observe as each stream of green light takes its natural course on the left and right thigh.

Feel the two streams relaxing the muscles in your left thigh and right thigh.

Feel the muscles relax.

(10 seconds)

Notice as the two streams drop further to your knees.

Feel it behind the knee caps.

Feel it carry the tension away from your knees.

Notice how your knee caps are feeling relaxed.

Feel all the muscles and veins in your knees relaxing.

(10 seconds)

Become aware of the two streams of green light drop to the lower parts of your legs.

Feel them relaxing the muscles in your calves.

Notice all the tension in your calves disappearing.

The green light flows into your shins easing any tension here.

Your lower limbs now feel relaxed and at ease.

(30 seconds)

Become aware of your ankles.

Scan for any tension or pain in your ankles.

Allow the two streams of green light to drop simultaneously to your ankles.

Notice your ankles relaxing.

Notice the green light-absorbing all the tension in your ankles.

(10 seconds)

The two streams of green light then flow into your feet taking away any tension.

(10 seconds)

Once again, envision the beam of green light flowing seamless through your body from the top of your head to your toes.

Notice as it rushes down to your body, filling it with the green light.

Feel as this light touches all the parts that need healing.

Think of any weakness in your body.

Think of the parts that are hurting.

Think of any part that has an injury.

Become aware of the green light touching those parts and healing them completely.

(30 seconds)

Your entire body is now flooded with this green light.

Feel it expanding your aura.

Feel it releasing energy that your aura requires.

Become aware of the glow in your aura, chakras, and your entire body.

Visualize your aura becoming complete with no imbalances or holes.

(30 seconds)

Feel as your body relaxes even more.

(10 seconds)

Your mind is calm and clear.

(10 seconds)

Rest in this calmness and centeredness for a while.

(90 seconds)

Take your awareness to your surroundings and your body.

Listen to your gentle breathing.

(5 seconds)

Listen to the sounds in the room.

(5 seconds)

Listen to the sounds far away.

(5 seconds)

Wiggle your fingers and toes.

(5 seconds)

Shake your head from left to right.

(5 seconds)

Move your shoulders up and down.

(5 seconds)

Gently open your eyes.

Welcome back to consciousness.

You are now ready to face the day with a relaxed mind and body.

Enjoy the rest of your day.

13. Guided visualization 6 (Guided imagery for centering and grounding).

You may practice this meditation in a seated position either on a chair or the ground.

Begin by finding your comfortable seated position. Adjust your body as need be until you are comfortable and alert.

(10 seconds)

Sense the support the chair, cushion or ground offers to the parts of the body that they are in contact with. Feeling that support, allow your pelvis and buttocks to ground down and your upper body to elongate in an alert and upright posture.

Your shoulders are directly stack over your hips and dropping downwards.

Rest your hands on your lap or knees.

Release the weight of the arms to gravity.

Gently close your eyes and begin to be aware of your entire body.

(10 seconds)

Your feet... legs...thighs...pelvis...lower back... upper back...shoulders...abdomen...ribs...chest.... arms... neck and head. Just being aware of yourself as a physical being.

(20 seconds)

Now bring your awareness to your breath, and the actual physical sensations that manifest when you breath. Feel each breath as it comes in and goes out...

(20 seconds)

Allow the breath to be just as it is, without trying to change or regulate it in any way.

(20 seconds)

Allow it to flow easily and naturally, in its own rhythm and pace, knowing you are breathing perfectly well right now.

(30 seconds)

Allow the body to be still and as you sit here feel a sense of dignity, a sense of resolve, a sense of being complete, whole, in this very moment, with your posture reflecting this sense of wholeness.

(45 seconds)
As you sit here in still calmness, bring to mind a magnificent mountain that you have either seen or one that you imagine.

Gradually allow your imagination of this mountain to come to focus.

Have an overall sense of the mountain's shape, high and low peaks, its base, it steep and gently sloping slopes as well as the large base of bedrock that the mountain is rooted in.

Notice how beautiful, unmoving and majestic the mountain is.

What other aspects of the mountain can you see? Maybe the highest peak is disappearing into the low hanging clouds, or there are streams and waterfalls cascading down the slopes of the mountain, some rocks are protruding on the slopes or a part of the mountain is covered with trees.

(30 seconds)

Now embody the qualities of the mountain. See yourself as a majestic, unmovable and still mountain. Just like the bedrock grounds the mountain, you are held firmly by the ground beneath your feet or bottoms.

(10 seconds)

Grounded in the sitting posture, your head becomes the lofty peak, supported by the rest of the body and affording a panoramic view.

Your shoulders and arms the sides of the mountain. Your bottoms and legs the solid base, rooted to your cushion or your chair. Experience in your body a sense of uplift from deep within your pelvis and spine.

(10 seconds)

With each breath, as you continue sitting, becoming a little more a breathing mountain, alive and vital, yet unwavering in your inner stillness, completely what you are, beyond words and thought, a centered, grounded, unmoving presence.

(10 seconds)

As you sit here, becoming aware of the fact that as the sun travels across the sky, the light and shadows and colors are changing virtually moment by moment in the mountain's stillness, and the surface teams up with life and activity... streams, melting snow, waterfalls, plants and wildlife.

(10 seconds)

As the mountain sits, seeing and feeling how night follows day and day follows night. The bright warming sun, followed by the cool night sky studded with stars, and the gradual dawning of a new day.

(10 seconds)
Through it all, the mountain just sits, experiencing change in each moment, constantly changing, yet always just being itself.
It remains still as the seasons flow into one another and as the weather changes moment by moment and day by day, calmness abiding all change.

(10 seconds)

In summer, there is no snow on the mountain except perhaps for the very peaks or in crags shielded from direct sunlight. In the fall, the mountain may wear a coat of brilliant fire colors. In winter, a blanket of snow and ice.

(10 seconds)

In any season, it may find itself at times enshrouded in clouds or fog or pelted by freezing rain. People may come to see the mountain and comment on how beautiful it is or how it's not a good day to see the mountain, that it's too cloudy or rainy or foggy or dark.
None of these matter to the mountain, which remains at all times its essential self.

Clouds may come and clouds may go, tourists may like it or not. The mountain's magnificence and beauty are not changed one bit by whether people see it or not, seen or unseen, in sun or clouds, broiling or frigid, day or night. It just sits, being itself.

(10 seconds)

At times visited by violent storms, buffeted by snow and rain and winds of unthinkable magnitude. Through it all, the mountain sits. Spring comes, trees leaf out, flowers bloom in the high meadows and slopes, birds sing in the trees once again.

(10 seconds)

Streams overflow with the waters of melting snow. Through it all, the mountain continues to sit, unmoved by the weather, by what happens on its surface, by the world of appearances... remaining its essential self, through the seasons, the changing weather, the activity ebbing and flowing on its surface.

(10 seconds)

 In the same way, as you sit in meditation, you learn to experience the mountain, you embody the same central, unwavering stillness and roundedness in the face of everything that changes in your life, over seconds, over hours, over years.

You experience constantly the changing nature of mind and body and of the outer world, you have periods of light and darkness, activity and inactivity, moments of color and moments of darkness. You experience storms of varying intensity and violence in the outer world, mind and body and through it all you remain deeply rooted and grounded.

(10 seconds)

By embodying the mountain, you can emulate its strength and stability as your own. You can personify its energy to support you so that you encounter each moment with mindfulness, equanimity and clarity.

You will begin to understand and know that your thoughts, feelings, perceptions, emotional crises and everything else that happen is like the ever-changing weather and you are like the magnificent mountain. Ultimately you will come to know a deep stillness and wisdom.

(60 seconds)

May you know your strength, may you find equanimity and may you be grounded and centered.

(60 seconds)

Begin to gently deepen your breath. Wiggle your fingers and your toes. When you are ready gently open your eyes.

14. Guided visualization 7 (Guided imagery for calm and peace).

Find a quiet place where you can sit either on the ground with your legs crossed or on a chair with your feet on the ground.
Rest your hands on your lap.

(5 seconds)

Adjust your posture to lengthen your spine and drop your shoulders.
Gently close your eyes.
Take a deep breath in and exhale slowly.

(10 seconds)

Another deep breath in and completely empty your lungs.

(10 seconds)

With each breath let tension melt away from your body.

(20 seconds)

Continue to breathe deeply.

(20 seconds)

Take a deep breath, hold it for a few seconds then release it slowly.

(5 seconds)

Keep breathing deeply in and out.

(20 seconds)

Become aware of the top of your head.

Imagine relaxation flowing from the top of your head and spreading throughout your whole body.

(5 seconds)

Feel your forehead and eyes relaxing.

Notice your jaws releasing tension and softening.
Feel your cheeks becoming warm.

(10 seconds)

Notice as the peaceful sensation flows to your neck.
Feel it massaging your shoulder muscles and releasing tension.

Breathe in.
Breathe out.

(10 seconds)

Feel the peaceful sensation flowing to your arms.
Notice it soothing your arms, hands, and fingers.

(10 seconds)

Become aware of your mind relaxing as your body relaxes.
Notice how your thoughts seem weightless.

(10 seconds)

Observe as the peaceful sensation flows to your chest and belly.
Feel that area getting soothed and relaxed.
As your chest and belly rise with every inhale, it relaxes with every exhale.

(20 seconds)

Feel the peaceful sensation now caressing your back.
Notice all the tension being released from your back.

(10 seconds)

The peaceful sensation keeps flowing.
It is now relaxing your buttocks.

(10 seconds)

Visualize it flowing to your thighs.
It slides slowly to the back of your thighs.
It slides gently to the front of your thighs.
It relaxes your thighs completely.

(10 seconds)

The soothing sensation flows to your knees.
Feel it relaxing your knees.
Feel it softening the knee cap.

(10 seconds)

It picks its momentum and flows to your calves. Washing away any tension in your calves.

(5 seconds)

It slides into your shin.
It relieves all the tension lodged in your shin.
(10 seconds)

Become aware of your ankles.
Check for any strain or pain in your ankles.
Notice the peaceful sensation relaxing your ankles.

(10 seconds)

It now flows to your feet.
Notice it relaxing your feet.

(10 seconds)

Notice how your body feels calm and peaceful.

(30 seconds)

Envision yourself on a beach.
Notice the sun warming your face and body.
Feel the sand beneath your feet.

(5 seconds)

You are all alone on this beach.
It is serene
Listen to the sound of the ocean.

(10 seconds)

You notice a small boat on the shore and walk towards it.
Get into the boat and let the waves rock the boat into the waters.
You take a boat ride towards the island on the Far East.
Enjoying the sunshine and the breeze from the ocean.

(5 seconds)

You arrive at your destination and step out of the boat.
The sublime beauty of the island takes your breath

(5 seconds)

The view of the exotic birds and colored flowers.

(5 seconds)

The palm trees surrounding the island provide a scenic view.

(5 seconds)

In this place, you feel free and peaceful.
(10 seconds)

You notice a path leading into the heart of the island.
You follow it as you continue to soak up the beauty of the island.

(10 seconds)

At the center of the island, you notice a pool. You move towards it and undress before stepping into the waters.

(5 seconds)

With each step you take in to the pool, you feel more peaceful and calm.

(10 seconds)

You glide in the water and feel your thoughts melting away.

(10 seconds)

You are now peaceful and relaxed. You allow yourself to rest here and savor the beauty and serenity of this place.

(60seconds)

When you are ready to leave, you walk back to the boat, and ride back to the mainland bring along the peace and calm you experienced in the island.

(60seconds)

Slowly, become aware of your present moment.
Listen to your heartbeat.
Notice the warmth in your hands.
Wiggle your toes and fingers.
Gently open your eyes.

15. Guided visualization 8 (Guided imagery for relaxation).

This meditation is ideal for when you are looking for a quick go-to guided meditation for total body and mind relaxation. You can do it on its own or at the beginning of longer meditations to ground yourself and silence your mental chatter.

Find a comfortable and quiet place for your meditation. You may either sit on the ground with your legs crossed or on a chair with feet on the ground.

Take a deep and slow breath in. Hold your breath in and exhale completely emptying out your lungs.

Take another deep breath in, hold it in for as long as it feels comfortable and exhale all the air out.

Keep taking long and slow breaths. Hold your breath in and the exhale.

30 seconds

Allow yourself to let go tension and to relax with each deep breath.

60 seconds

Now, bring your awareness to the top of your head. Imagine a gentle, calming wave of relaxation beginning to flow downwards from the top of your head. It flows down to your forehead, the temples, the entire face, and the entire scalp as it softens your muscles and melts away tension.

Let the calming wave flow down your neck into your shoulders and arms. From the upper arms, elbows, forearms, wrists, palms, fingers, and the fingertips. As your breath in and out it becomes warmer and flows freely to sooth your muscles.

10 seconds

Your body is becoming more relaxed and your thoughts lighter.

10 seconds

The wave now flows to your chest and stomach.

10 seconds

Notice the gentle rise and fall of your belly and chest as your breath.

10 seconds

Bring your attention to your upper back and let the wave flow down your spin to the lower back. It relaxes all the muscles and organs in your torso.

10 seconds

Your entire upper body is loose, heavy and relaxed.

10 seconds

The calming wave works its way down your lower body relaxing the hips, buttocks, back of your thighs, front of your thighs, the knees, shins, calves, ankles, feet and all the 10 toes.

10 seconds

Allow the entire lower body to relax and become limb.

10 seconds

Allow the entire body to be completely relaxed. You are calm, still and peaceful.

30 seconds

Bask in this calmness for a few more long, relaxing breathes.

60 seconds

When you are ready, gently open your eyes and get on with the rest of your day.

Chapter 3: Happiness Meditation

This section contains guided smiling and gratitude meditations to help you feel joyful, contented and happy.

16. Gratitude Meditation

Find a comfortable and upright sitting position either on the ground, a cushion or a chair.

Take a deep breath in and a deep breath out.

(5 seconds)

At your own pace, take three more deep breaths allowing your mind to become present.

(30 seconds)

Now, resume natural breathing without intentionally making your breath deeper or shallower.

 (20 seconds)

Notice how effortless your breathing is. Notice the miracle that is your breathing.

(5 seconds)

You go about your day and in every moment, you are breathing. Your body knows what to do. You don't have to remind it to breath.

(5 seconds)

You heart knows when and how to beat. Your organs are doing their work and the various body systems are functioning well.

Isn't it magical?

(5 seconds)

Yet, it is easy to get caught up in everyday life and forget to be grateful for such miracles as your heart pumping, your brain functioning, the sun rising and setting and the divine order of life among others.

Practicing gratitude can help you to shift from a stressed mood to a happier, more contented mood.

(5 seconds)

Let's practice gratitude now.

Notice your body and express gratitude for it. No matter the shape or color of your body, it is the vessel that takes you through life.

Take your attention from head to toe as you say "thank you" to each body part.

(1 minute)

Express gratitude for your abilities, gifts, talents, and skills.

(15 seconds)

Your personality, strengths and weaknesses.

(15 seconds)

Be grateful for the various opportunities, insights and solutions that life offers you.

(15 seconds)

Your being here matters. You matter. You are worthy. You are enough.

(15 seconds)

Now express your gratitude for your home. It doesn't how matter big or small this place is. Or, whether you think you need to buy certain things or renovate.
This is the place you call home and at this moment it is enough.
Offer gratitude for the various aspects of your home.

(30 seconds)

Now, identify the people in your life that you are grateful for.

Your family

(10 seconds)

friends

(10 seconds)

lover or partner

(10 seconds)

and other people you encounter in your daily life

(10 seconds)

Take a few moments to notice what else you are grateful for.

(30 seconds)

Now notice how you feel and bring that calm joy into your day.

May you be happy,
may you be peaceful,
may you be harmonious.

Love and light to you.

17. Smiling Meditation 1

Find a comfortable place where you can sit silently for the next few minutes.
Sit up straight with your spine lengthened.
Gently close your eyes and bring your attention to your breath.
The following breathing exercise will help your body and mind to relax.

Breathe in for a count of 4, hold the breath for a count of 4 and then exhale slowly for a count of 8.

Breathe in for a count of 4, hold the breath for a count of 4 and then exhale slowly for a count of 8.

Breathe in for a count of 4, hold the breath for a count of 4 and then exhale slowly for a count of 8.

Breathe in for a count of 4, hold the breath for a count of 4 and then exhale slowly for a count of 8.

Again, repeat this process, breathing in for a count of 4, holding the breath for the count of 4 and then breathing out for the count of 8.

Now bring your attention to our face. Notice if you are holding any tension on your jaws, eyes, forehead or any other part of the face.

(10 seconds)

If you notice tension in any part of your face breath energy into it. Imagine a relaxing white energy shining on that part as it melts away the tension. Breath out deeply and allow the tension to leave your body.

(10 seconds)

Let the relaxing white light fill your entire face as it softens and relaxes the face. Allow you jaw, cheeks, lips, nose, eyes and forehead to completely relax.

(10 seconds)

Allow your lips and cheeks to relax into a gentle smile. Think of something amusing or someone you love and let your heart fill with joy.

(10 seconds)

Continue to focus on the happy memory as you smile.

If there is tension in your body, allow the joy of the smile to wash over the tensed part of the body. Let all your muscles relax and soften.

(10 seconds)

Stay in the tensed part of the body until it relaxes fully. When that part of the body is relaxed, move on to the next tight part of the body.

(45 seconds)

Now, smile into all the muscles and cells of the body and allow your entire body to relax.

(30 seconds)

Bring your attention into your heart and as you smile let it fill up with joy and happiness.

(10 seconds)

Visualize your heart charka opening or pulsating and expanding with love energy. The heart energy is a green light. The green light represent love. Hold this focus for a few minutes, focusing on the love in your heart center.

(90 seconds)

Bring even more joy into your body and mind by reciting the following affirmations:

I am happy and relaxed

I smile often

I find it easy to be happy

I choose to be happy

When I smile the world responds by bringing more joyful circumstances into my life.

(15 seconds)

Bring your awareness back to your face. Notice how you feel happier and lighter.

(15 seconds)

As you end this meditation, always know that you can bring more joy into your life by simply smiling.

Take a deep breath and as you exhale slowly open your eyes.

18. Smiling Meditation 2

How often do you go about you go about your day with along face? Fatigue, stress and disconnection are spelt out on your face. You rarely smile. You take everything too seriously and it is not helping your mood.

A simple smile on your face can instantly improve your mood, boost your energy and make you feel connected with yourself and other people.

You can practice this meditation anytime and anywhere. At any one point, check in with yourself, and gently pull your cheeks backwards.

Let's practice the smiling meditation

Come to a seated position with your spine tall and lengthened.
Gently close your eyes.
Notice any noise and sounds are around you and your body.

15 seconds

Now bring your attention inwards. Take a moment to notice what is happening with you, your feelings, emotions, sensations and energy.

30 seconds

Now notice your breathing

15 seconds

Take a long deep breath, filling up the lungs. Hold your breath in and gently exhale slowly releasing the breath. Another deep breath in, hold and long exhale.

Allow your breath to assume it natural pattern and let yourself relax.

30 seconds

Let go of any expectations, should haves, would haves and could haves.

15 seconds

Stay in the awareness of your senses. Pay attention to your skin, nose, ears, eyes and the taste in the mouth.

1minute

Listen to your heart beat. Energetically, is it numb, vulnerable, open or closed? Observe without any judgment.
20 seconds

Now, relax your face as you breath. Pull your cheeks backwards and put a gentle smile in your face.

10 seconds

Keep the smile and notice the energy of your body. Did your heart open slightly? Do you feel happier?
Notice how this smile affects your energy, emotions, feelings and sensations.

Allow the smile to spread to your checks, the corners of your eyes and entire face. Let the smile grow to your entire body. Notice how it feels to smile. Feel the muscles on your mouth as they move.

30 seconds

Take a deep breath and relax your face. In the next breath come to a full smile. Notice how wonderful it is to feel happy and positive.

30 seconds

Let your whole face bask in the smile. Imagine your heart smiling. It is filled with vibrant and happy energy

30 seconds

Bring the joy and happiness to your tummy, legs and the whole body.

30 seconds

Enjoy the sense of ease, bliss and joy.

1 minute

Let your whole body feel positive, happy and contented.

1 minute

Take a deep breath in and set an intention to bring this ease and bliss to your day and life. Exhale out and bring your awareness back to the room.

Chapter 4: Body Awareness & Body Scan Meditations

Body scan meditation is a foundational meditation technique that helps you to still your mind chatter, relief mental stress, release muscular tension, and cultivate an awareness of your body. It offers you an "in-the-body" experience as you move your attention from one part of the body to another.

During your practice, you may encounter a wide range of sensations including but not limited to pain, heaviness, tingling, heat, warmth, cold, lightness, itchiness, or no sensations at all. It is possible that one part of the body may present more than one type of sensations at a time. Even when you scan through your body for a second time, it is likely that the same body part will exhibit different sensations from the first time. Your mind, due to the habit of constantly judging, will interpret these sensations as either pleasant or unpleasant. Make a deliberate and consistent effort to remain non-judgmental of the sensations. Observe them for what they are without labelling them.

The body-scan meditation leads to a deep relaxation of both the mind and the body. It is best to do it in a lying down position to provide a conducive posture for deep relaxation.

The intention of this type of meditation is to spend time with each part of the body, cultivating an awareness of what is happening there. Let go off any expectations on the outcomes of this meditation and just be here. Follow along the instructions as best as you can. You mind will occasionally wander. Notice it and gently bring back your awareness to the body.

19. Body scan meditation 1 (Technique: body awareness)

Assume a comfortable seated position with your spine lengthened and shoulders relaxed. Take a deep breath in through your nose and exhale out through your mouth. Again, inhale through your nose and hold your breath in. With your mouth closed, exhale out and hold your breath out. Inhale through your nose, hold your breath in, exhale through the nose, hold your breath out.
Repeat this technique a few more times.

(I minute)

Now, resume normal breathing rhythm and notice your breath and as it comes in and out through your nose.

(30 seconds)

Using your five senses, we are going to pay effortless attention to your body.

Notice any parts of your body that are in contact with each other or the ground. Your buttocks on the ground or chair, your hands on the thighs, the contact between your crisscrossed legs, and your feet on the ground.

Notice the warmth at the contact point between your hands and the thighs.
Does the chair feel hard and warm? Or maybe it is hard and cold.

If you are sitting on a cushion, notice the gentle compression of the cushion as your buttocks press it downwards.

How does the ground beneath your feet feel? Hard? Soft, cold, maybe warm. Remain aware without changing anything.

(15 seconds)

Now, bring your attention to your mouth. Is there is taste in your tongue?

Is you jaw clenched or relaxed?

Are your upper and lower teeth together or apart?

Is your tongue touching the top roof of your mouth or resting between the lower set of your teeth?

Are your lips tightly sealed or slightly apart?

(15seconds)

Now, notice any smell. May be the air around you is clean and odorless. Or, there is a strong pleasant or maybe not pleasant smell. Notice any sensations around your nostrils.

(15 seconds)

Bring your attention to your ears.

Notice any sounds, loud or not so loud. First within the room you are in then any noises in your house and in the nearby surroundings.
Notice any silence too.

(15 seconds)

Take your attention to your eyes. Are they tightly closed or gently closed? Can you sense light or darkness on your eyelids?

(15 seconds)

Stay in this calm awareness as you gently breath in and out.

(30seconds)

When you are ready, gently open your eyes, notice your surroundings and get on with the rest of your day.

May you be happy,
may you be peaceful,
may you be harmonious.

Love and light to you

20. Body Scan Meditation 2 (Body Awareness)

Find a comfortable place where you can lie down.

Lie on your back and extend your feet forward.

Draw your chin away from your chest and drop your shoulders away from your ears.

Place your arms a few inches away from your body palms facing up with fingers slightly separated.

Separate your feet hip width apart or slightly wider, whichever feels most comfortable for you.

Allow the feet to drop towards the ground in the opposite directions.

Take a deep breath in and a deep breath out.

(5 seconds)

Once again breath in deeply and as you exhale allow your body to relax completely.

(5 seconds)

Keep breathing in and out allowing your body to relax completely.

(30 seconds)

Now, bring your attention to your feet.

Notice both big toes and the other toes on both feet. Notice the soles of your feet, your heels and the tops of your feet.

(5 seconds)

Notice your ankles, your shins and your calves.

(5 seconds)

Take your attention to your knees, right thigh and then the left thigh.

(5 seconds)

Notice your pelvic area: the groin, hips and the buttocks.

(5 seconds)

Notice the lower back, the middle back, and the upper back.

(5 seconds)

Your belly, your ribs and your chest.

(5 seconds)

Take your attention to your fingers: the thumbs, index fingers, middle fingers, ring fingers and small fingers.

(5 seconds)

Notice the back side of your palms then the front side of your palms.

(5 seconds)

Take your attention to your wrists, forearms and elbows.

(5 seconds)

Shift your awareness to the biceps, triceps and shoulders.

(5 seconds)

The front and back of your neck.

(5 seconds)

From the back of the neck, draw your attention upwards to the entire scalp.

(5 seconds)

Notice your forehead, the eyebrows, the space between your eyebrows, and your eyelids.
Notice your ears and nose, your cheeks and jaws, your upper lip and lower lip, and your teeth and tongue.

(5 seconds)

Become aware of your entire body.

(30 seconds)

Now, randomly move your attention to the various parts of the body.

Your armpits, inner thighs and heels.

Notice your fingers, belly button and toes.

The wrists, elbows and knees.

Keep moving your attention randomly across your body.

(1 minute)

You are relaxed, calm and present. Lie in this stillness as you observe your body

(1 minute)

Begin to deepen your breath.

(15 seconds)

Wiggle your fingers and toes Make circles with your wrists and ankles.

(5 seconds)

Straighten your hands past your head. Stretch like you are being pulled on both sides.

(5 seconds)

Hug your knees to your chest tightly.

(5 seconds)

Roll over to your right-hand side.

(5 seconds)

Stay here for a few seconds

(15 seconds)

When you are ready sit up. Take a few moments of silence before getting on with the rest of your day.

May you be happy,
may you be peaceful,
may you be harmonious.

Love and light to you

21. Body Scan Mediation 3 (Muscle contraction for total body and mind relaxation)

Lie down with your feet extended to the front and hands resting alongside your body, palms facing up.
Gentle close your eyes.
Take a deep breath in and as you exhale let go the weight of your body to the surface beneath.
Take another deep breath and as you exhale let go any thoughts you are having.

Take one more breath in, hold your breath in for a moment as you allow the air to infiltrate every cell of your body.
Exhale, and let go any tension that your body is holding.

Now take your attention to your feet, tighten your feet muscles as much as you can and then release allowing all the tension on your feet to go.

Tighten your right leg muscles and release.

Tighten your left leg muscles and release.

Tighten the thighs and release.

Tighten the right buttock and release.

Tighten the left buttock and release.

Tighten both buttocks and release.

Tighten all the muscles on both legs from the feet up to the buttocks, and release.

Become aware of the entire lower body dissipating stress and tension.

(20 seconds)

Now tighten the belly and release

Tighten the chest and release
Tighten the lower back muscles and release

Tighten the upper back muscles and release

Make tight fists with your hands and release

Tighten your arms and release

Tighten the neck and release

Scan through your scalp and release and tension you may be holding there.

Clench your jaw, tightly seal you lips and eye lids and then release.

Allow your body to completely relax and to be heavy.

(20 seconds)

Notice any physical sensations in your body. Some sensations may be obvious, while others might be subtle.

Your entire body may feel heavy. Whatever sensations are on your body, notice them.

(30 seconds)

Notice how your entire body is calm and relaxed.

(30 seconds)

Allow yourself to enjoy this state of a tension-free body and a relaxed mind.

(1 minute)

Allow yourself to become restful

(1 minute)

Take a deep breath in and as you exhale, gently wiggle your fingers and your toes, and make circles with your hands and your writs.

Notice your surroundings and when you are ready, get up and get on with the rest of your day.

22. Body Scan Mediation 4 (Body awareness for total body and mind relaxation)

Find a comfortable place to lie down.
Lie down on you back with the body straight, hands besides your hips palms facing up. Let your feet fall naturally to the sides facing away from each other.

Take a deep breath in and breath out. Another breath in and out. Notice your body on the floor.

Take your attention to your feet. What sensation is here right now on the toes, soles, feet. Notice whether or not there are sensations. Are the subtle or gross? Remain with the awareness with your feet.

20 seconds

Shift your awareness to the ankles. Then the lower left leg, the left calf muscle, the back of the knee, the knee caps, the left hamstring. The left quad, left hip, left buttock

10 seconds

Be aware of the contact between you left leg with floor. Hold that awareness in patience and equanimity. Without judging but accepting all the sensations as they are.

20 seconds

Now, take your attention to the right ankle. The lower right leg, the right calf muscle, the back of the knee, the knee caps, the right hamstring. The right quad, right hip, right buttock.

20 seconds

Be aware of the contact between you right leg with floor. Hold that awareness in patience and equanimity. Without judging but accepting all the sensations as they are.

30 seconds

Become aware of the groin, the pubic bone and the entire pelvis.

20 seconds

Remain in awareness of both legs. Take a deep breath and sense the sensations of both legs from the skin to muscles, to the bones and the inside of your legs, thighs and butts. Remain with what is the truth for you here.

30 seconds

Take a deep breath in and imagine the breath filling your legs and then breath out. Take another deep breath and do the same. Notice any changes in sensations in the lower body.

30 seconds

You may find yourself feeling bored, restless or wanting to move faster. This is normal. Simply notice the feelings and remain Equanimeous. Slightly deepen your breath to help you stay in the awareness and to bring your attention back to your body.

30 seconds.

Now take your awareness to your lower back. Gradually take your attention to the middle back and upper back including the shoulders. Take your attention to the spine from the lower spine to the base of the neck. Hold the entire back in awareness.

30 seconds

Take your attention to the front of the body. At the lower abdomen, belly, rib cages, chest, breast, collar bone What sensations are in the front upper part of the body?

30 seconds

Shift your attention to the left hand. The left-hand fingers, backs of the palms, palms, wrist, fore arm, elbow, upper arm, biceps, triceps, shoulder. Hold the left hand in awareness.

20 seconds

Then to the right hand, The right-hand fingers, backs of the palms, palms, wrist, forearm, elbow, upper arm, biceps, triceps, shoulder. Hold the left hand in awareness.

20 seconds

Hold both hands in awareness.

30 seconds

And now to the front of your neck, back of your neck, your scalp, both ears, crown of your head, forehead, eyebrows, both eyes, cheeks, nose, upper lip, lower lip and chin. Pay attention to your entire face.

30 seconds

Take a deep breath and as you exhale, take your attention to your mouth. Your teeth, tongue, jaw, and top of your mouth.

30 seconds

Take a deep breath in and imagine energy flowing from your head to your feet, and as you exhale empty out. In the next inhale, hold the breath in, let it flow in the whole body and exhale allowing the body lets go tension.

Now lie down, allowing your body to be as it is. Resting in awareness, from moment to moment. Letting yourself be as you are in this moment. With no judgments, nowhere to go, nothing to do, see, say or here. Just lying down in calm awareness.

2 minutes

Now bring your attention to the right-hand palm, crown of your head, left sole of your feet, back of your neck, right armpit, left thigh, right knee, nose and forehead.

Notice any feelings of restlessness, boredom or need to move the attention faster. Take a deep breath hold breathe in and let go.

Bring your attention to your shoulders, belly button, buttocks, both ankles, genitals, right elbow, elbows, years and crown of your head. Take a deep breath in and a deep breath out.

Sweep attention through the front part of your body from your forehead, your face, neck, chest, belly, pelvic bone, front of your thighs, knees and feet.

Sweep your attention from the back of your head, neck, back, buttocks, thighs, calves, shins, and heels.

Hold the entire body in awareness.

2 minutes

Become are of your left foot.
The left big toe, the second toe, third toe, forth toe, fifth toe, the nails, top part of your toes, space between your toes. Spread the attention to the entire sole of your right foot, the balls of the feet, the middle of the foot, the heel, the sides of the foot, the top of the left foot, the ankles.

10 seconds

Now, take your attention to your right leg, the shin muscles, calf, front of the knee, back of the knee, front of the thigh, back of the thigh, inner thigh, outer thigh, hips, and right buttock.

10 seconds

Bring your attention to the left leg. The shin muscles, calf, front of the knee, back of the knee, front of the thigh, back of the thigh, inner thigh, outer thigh, hips, and left buttock.

10 seconds

Become aware of your belly, the belly button, ribs, and the entire chest.

10 seconds

Become aware of the sides of your body.

10 seconds

Take your attention to your lower back, the entire spinal column from the bottom of your back to the bottom of your neck. The lower back, mid back and upper back.

10 seconds

Now take your attention to the backside of the neck.

10 seconds

Spread that awareness to your scalp and top of your head.

10 seconds

Become aware of your forehead, the eyebrows, space between your eyebrows, the eyes, eyes lids and eye lashes.

10 seconds

Your right ear, right cheek, nose, left cheek, left ear. The jaw, the chin, upper lip and lower lip.

10 seconds

Bring your attention to your mouth, the roof of the mouth, the tongue and the teeth.

10 seconds

Allow your lips to part slightly and for the tongue to rest between the teeth on the lower side of the mouth.

10 seconds

Let your eyes draw backwards and downwards as you relax your eyelids.

10 seconds

Become aware of your entire body lying heavily on the surface beneath.

3 minutes

Take a deep breath in and a deep breath out.

10seconds

Pay attention to the room you are in -: any sounds, or noise.

10 seconds

Gently wiggle your fingers and your toes. Hug your knees to your chest and roll over to the right side.

10 seconds

Gently come up to sitting with your legs crossed. Take a deep breath in and out. Notice how your body feels. May the calm and peace you feel flow into your life.

Chapter 5: Intention Setting Meditation

A simple guided meditation that can be done in the morning or at the beginning of an activity to set an intention and focus your energy.

23.Intention Setting Meditation

Come to comfortable, alert and upright position sitting
position.
Find some level of ease in your posture.
When you are ready, gently close your eyes.

Take a deep breath in and a deep breath out.
Notice your surroundings: the sounds, temperatures.

15 seconds

Now bring your attention to your body. Your natural
breath, sensations, feelings, and mood. Settle into this
moment. Settle into the here and now.

30 seconds

Notice your normal natural breathing.

30 seconds

follow your breath as it comes in and as it goes out.

30 seconds

Allow the natural flow of your breath to be your resting
place

30 seconds

Today's meditation will focus on intention setting. Setting
intentions incorporates a balance of focusing on what you

want to create and surrender. It is putting your intentions out to the universe and trusting that it will conspire to fulfill your heart wishes. That it will support you. It is shifting from what you want to do and determining your way of being.

I will guide you through some questions and allow you some time to think about to help you set intention for your life and this day.

What really matters to you?
30 seconds

What

What fears would you like to release?

 30 seconds

What do you want to do better?

30 seconds

In what areas of your life do you want to be better?

30 seconds

What daily practices can you incorporate to remain anchored in your life?

30 seconds

What do you want to accomplish today? Identify the things you want to do.

30 seconds

Identify the why of the action. For instance, if one of the things on your to-do list is grocery shopping. Then the why is to provide healthy meals for my family or live a healthy lifestyle.

30 seconds

Beyond what you get to do today, who do you choose to be today? What are the values do you choose live by today? For example, to be strong, kind, deliberate, empathetic, to enjoy life, and to be present among others.

30 seconds

How do you want to show up to life today?

30 seconds

Who do you choose to be in life? What values do you choose to live by?

30 seconds

Who are you grateful?

30 seconds

What are you grateful for?

How do you want to show up to life today?

30 seconds

Bring your attention back to your body. Take deep breath in and out.

10 seconds

Take a few more deep breaths in and out.

30seconds

Brings the outer edges of your hands to touch and place them in front of you.
Reaffirm your intentions with the following statement. My intention is…. (to be present).
Note the tasks you want to do today. Note your fears, challenges, and questions.

Now blow all the intentions to your palm. Place your palms on your chest. Letting your intentions, questions, fears and plans to dissolve into your heart. Your heart is intuitive and knows what you need and how to accomplish it. Trust that it will figure out things for your highest good.

Take a deep breath in and a deep breath out. Bring the outer edges of your hands to touch and place them in front of your chest. Now blow your intentions into the universe. With a sense of surrender and trust.

Place yours hands on your laps, take a deep breath in and out. Slowly open your eyes. With a gentle smile notice your surroundings and getting on with the rest of your day.

Chapter 6: Self- Healing Meditation

Our nature as human beings is that we are not perfect.

Often times, we fall short of what we expect of ourselves or others. We break the rules, make mistakes, and mess up. We expect others to meet our expectations, be in their best behavior and act in a certain way.

Despite our knowing that none of us is perfect, we hold grudges against others when they wrong us, and feel embarrassed, guilty and ashamed of ourselves when we make mistakes. Usually, carrying this guilt around and allowing the mistake to define us. This takes away our ability our best life, now.

Forgive yourself. Forgive others. Be compassionate with yourself and others. Let go the baggage you are carrying of your past mistakes. Fix what can be fixed about a situation. Show remorse and ask for forgiveness whenever possible. Take any action that can be made to improve the situation. And let go the shame and guilt. Realize that while someone may have wronged you in one instance or another, carrying that guilt around robs you more than it gives you in your life.

At times, it can be really difficult to forgive. In such cases, setting an intention to forgive sets the ball rolling. It may take several days, maybe months and in some cases even years to let go. But setting the intention and reaffirming it, allows you to offload some of the baggage.

Self-healing meditation can be done on a daily basis to let go the baggage of resentment on a day to day basis. Or, any time when you feel overwhelmed with anger, bitterness, shame or guilt.

24. Guided meditation for forgiveness and compassion

Find a comfortable and upright seated position.
Take a deep breath in and a deep breath out.
Take three more deep inhales and exhales

30 seconds

Place your right hand on your heart center.
Notice the chest rising and falling.

30 seconds

Feel the energy of your heart. Does it feel heavy, light or maybe in between?

30 seconds

Affirm to yourself that I completely, love and accept myself three times.

15 seconds

Now, bring to mind something that you did that you feel either guilty, embarrassed or ashamed about.

15 seconds

Say to yourself, "I acknowledge that I am not perfect. I forgive myself for this situation." Repeat at least three times

30 seconds

Bring to mind any other situations or things you did that you feel bad about.
And again say "I acknowledge that I am not perfect and I forgive myself"

30 seconds

If you find it difficult to directly forgive yourself, say "I am willing to forgive myself". Repeat it least 3 times

30 seconds

We are our own critics, in some cases, we are worse critics than other people are of us.
Let yourself off the hook and allow yourself to be kind and compassionate to yourself. Offer yourself unconditional love.

30 seconds

Now bring to mind someone that has wronged you.
Notice how much pain they have caused you.

10 seconds

Realize that they too are not perfect. And, even if they did you wrong intentionally, it doesn't serve you to keep carrying their burden.
They are offering you a gift of pain, disrespect and any other bad you feel they are causing you.
You can either receive it or refuse to take it.

10 seconds

I know it is easier said than done to offer forgiveness to others. At times, it may feel like you are offering them good that they do not deserve by forgiving them. Do it for yourself.

10 seconds

Say, "I am willing to forgive this person or situation"

10 seconds
"I forgive (mention the person's name)"

10 seconds

"I take back my power and withdraw my energy and attention from (mention person's name) or (the situation)"

10 seconds

"I understand that healing is a process and I am willing to start it now."

10seconds

Repeat the forgiveness affirmations:

"I am willing to forgive this person or situation"

10 seconds
"I forgive (mention the person's name)"

10 seconds

"I take back my power and withdraw my energy and attention from (mention person's name) or (the situation)"

10 seconds

"I understand that healing is a process and I am willing to start it now."

10seconds

Repeat one more time:

"I am willing to forgive this person or situation"

10 seconds
"I forgive (mention the person's name)"

10 seconds

"I take back my power and withdraw my energy and attention from (mention person's name) or (the situation)"

10 seconds

"I understand that healing is a process and I am willing to start it now."

10seconds

Now, take some deep breaths into your heart center.

20 seconds

Let the deep breaths bring cleansing energy into your heart and as you exhale, let the air leaving your body carry away your pain and heaviness.

1 minute

Notice as your heart rises and falls against your right hand.

30 seconds

Affirm "I am willing to be kind and compassionate to myself. I let go myself criticism. I am willing and open to let go the baggage of resentment I am carrying"

I am willing to be kind and compassionate to myself. I let go myself criticism. I am willing and open to let go the baggage of resentment I am carrying"

I am willing to be kind and compassionate to myself. I let go myself criticism. I am willing and open to let go the baggage of resentment I am carrying"

Notice how you feel now. Maybe you feel lighter or you feel resistance to the ideal of letting go and forgiving. That is fine. Say to yourself, "no matter how I feel, I completely love and accept myself". Staying in this knowing.

30 seconds

Take one more deep breath and as you exhale, release your hand.

Comeback to your normal natural breathing.

20 seconds

Gently open your eyes.

25.Guided meditation for deep emotional self-healing

As we grow up, both the society and the education system put an emphasis on taking care of our bodies. We are encouraged to eat healthily, exercise and seek medical help when the body is not well. But we are not taught how to take care of our emotions yet emotional pain is inevitable.

What do you do when your heart is broken, or you feel rejected? How do you deal with the emotional pain of failure, rejection, loss, grief, loneliness, anxiety, anger and other painful emotions?

This guided meditation will help you to heal some of your emotional wounds. You can practice it over and over and as frequently as you need to, to overcome and deal with your emotional pain.

Let's get started

Identify a comfortable and quiet space where you can lie down.
Lie die on your back with your feet hip-width or wider and hands resting alongside your body palms facing up.
Take a deep breath in and as you exhale gently close your eyes.

Continue to take deep breaths, inhaling through your nose and exhaling through your mouth.

20 seconds

With every inhale, completely fill up your lungs and with every exhale completely empty out.

30 seconds

Inhale deeply through your nose, exhale completely through your mouth

1 minute

Now close your mouth and breathe deeply in and out through your mouth.

30 seconds

Completely fill up your lungs and completely empty out.

30 seconds

Now, pay attention to your belly, as you breath in let your belly rise and completely fill up and as you exhale allow your belly to empty out and fall.

1 minute

Pay attention to your chest, as you breath in let your chest rise and completely fill up and as you exhale allow your chest to empty out and fall.

1 minute

Keep breathing deeply, paying attention to both your chest and belly as the air comes in and goes out.

1 minute

Now bring your attention to your right leg. Tighten it from the toes, up the ankle, shin and calf, knee to the thigh. Make each muscle on the right leg tight and then tighter until they can't get any tighter. Hold that tension in for a bit and now release and relax the entire right leg. Allow all the tension, physical and emotional you hold on your right leg to melt away.

10 seconds

Bring your attention to your left leg. Tighten it from the toes, up the ankle, shin and calf, knee to the thigh. Make each muscle on the left leg tight and then tighter until they can't get any tighter. Hold that tension in for a bit and now release and relax the entire left leg. Allow all the tension, physical and emotional you hold on you left leg to melt away.

10 seconds

You may make any movements with your legs to help them relax more. Wiggle your toes, roll your ankles, draw your feet, knees and thighs towards each other and then apart. Let both legs rest and be fully support by the surface beneath them. They are relaxed.

20 seconds

Bring your attention to your buttocks. Squeeze them tightly and then tighter. Now, relax them allowing the muscles to let go.

10 Seconds

Take your attention to your abdomen area. Tense all the muscles here and then relax.

10 seconds

Suck your belly in and the push it out. Repeat this four more times.

20 seconds

Take a full deep breath into your belly and the empty all the air out. Repeat this breathing technique three more times

30 seconds

Allow your abdominal muscles to fully relax.

10 seconds

Draw your shoulders to the front towards the center of your chest to contract the chest muscles. Contract in more and the release allowing the entire front side of your body to relax.

10 seconds

Now, draw your shoulder blades towards each other contacting all your back muscles. Pull them closer and squeeze your back muscles tighter. Then release and allow the entire back to relax.

10 seconds

Focus your attention on your left arm. Make tight fist and tighten all the arm muscles up to the shoulders. Make them tighter and then release allowing your entire left hand to relax.

10 seconds

Focus your attention on your right arm. Make a tight fist and tighten all the arm muscles up to the shoulders. Make them tighter and then release allowing your entire left hand to relax.

10 seconds

Now, wiggle the fingers of both hands, make circles with your wrist and move your arms side to side. Gently shake off any tension held on your hands and let the rest and relax on the surface beneath.

10 seconds

Let the entire torso and arms relax completely.

10 seconds

Let the weight of your torso and lower body sink into the surface beneath allowing you to relax and let go.

10 seconds

Take a few deep breaths in and out through your nose.

30 seconds

Draw your chin to your chest and tighten the muscles in front of your neck as you lengthen those at the back of your neck. Squeeze a little bit more and then release allowing your neck to relax.

10 seconds

Now bring your attention to your face. Tightly close your eyes and lips, and clench your jaw. Tightly squeeze all your facial muscles, and the release letting your face to relax.

10 seconds

Now tighten as many muscles of your body as you can. From your toes to your head. Point your toes towards your shins, pull your knee caps up, squeeze your buttocks, suck your belly in, make tight fists, draw your chin to your chest, clench your jaw and shut your eyes tightly. Tighten the muscles more. Take a deep breath in, hold your breath and then open your mouth, sigh out as you relax all your muscles.

20 seconds

Let your entire body lie still.

20 seconds

Now, take a deep inhale and let it infiltrate every cell of your body and as you exhale allow the breath to leave your body taking with it any tension that is still in your body.

Repeat this breathing technique three more times.

1 minute

Now visualize a white light entering your body through the center of the soles of your feet. It is a warm, cleansing and calming energy. It infiltrates all the cells of your body from your feet, up your ankles, legs, knees, thighs, pelvis, entire torso, arms, neck, head and face.

Upon reaching the top of your head, it begins to flow downwards from your head, to your neck, arms, entire torso, pelvis, legs down to your feet. Cleansing and melting away all the tension in your body.

It keeps flowing from your toes to your head and back to the toes.

1 minute

Now, the light leaves your body through the top of your head. It creates an aura of calm and serene energy around you before dissolving back into the universe.

20 seconds

Assume your normal natural breathing. Do not make it deeper or shallower. Let it assume its own rhythm and pattern.

20 seconds

You body is lying down calm, still and peaceful.

20 seconds

Now, bring to mind something that is weighing heavy in your heart. It could be someone, something or a situation. It can be a relationship, an embarrassing moment, a mistake you made or someone else offended you. It may have happened now or a long time ago.

 A number of things may be weighing you down. Choose the one that comes first or the one that you feel is causing you the most emotional pain.

20 seconds

Throughout this process, make an intention to remain still. Your body may become restless due to the emotional discomfort that thinking and dealing with hurtful situations and the emotions they bring come with them. If you feel distracted and restless, stay with the process but deepen your breath to keep you grounded.

5 seconds

Allow yourself to remember the details of what is weighing you down.

What happened?

Where were you?

What were you wearing.

Who else was there?

See all the details and allow the emotions to come up.

20 seconds

Can you identify the emotions you are feeling? Maybe you feel bitter and resentful, or angry, betrayed, embarrassed, lonely, sad, confused or any other emotions.

15 seconds

Where does the emotion manifest in your body? Pay attentions to the sensations in your body to be able to tell where the emotion manifests. If there is more than one emotion, focus on the most conspicuous.

15 seconds

At this moment, it is ok to feel the emotions. Do not judge and label them as unpleasant or bad. Just observe them objectively. As energy.

15 seconds

If the emotion were a color, what color is it? Do not overthink it, go with the color that comes up first.

5 seconds

What is its temperature. Is it hot, warm or cold?

5 seconds

Ask of the energy what message or lesson it has for you for your highest good.

15 seconds

Ask what truths do you need to see

15 seconds

Ask any other follow up questions that may come up

30 seconds

Keep breathing deeply and with ease as you allow the emotions to come up.

1 minute

Now imagine all the emotions, thoughts and memories you feel about this situation collecting at your heart center to form a dark cotton-like ball.

The ball leaves your body and begins to drift upwards. It keeps drifting into the clouds and gets dissolved into the sky.

As you watch the ball of energy drift away, you get a sense that you are safe. You now know that you are not attached to the thoughts, memories and feelings of the situation. You know that these emotions no longer have control on you.

30 seconds

Now notice how much lighter and happier you feel.

I will allow you some time to stay here, feeling calm, light, peaceful and grounded

5 minutes

Now begin to deepen your breath.

10 seconds

Wiggle your fingers and toes. Make circles with your wrists and ankles. Stretch and hug both knees to your chest.

10 seconds

When you are ready sit up right with your legs crossed. Take three deep breaths.

30 seconds

Listen to what is happening around you and gently open your eyes.

26.Guided meditation for letting go hurts by other people

Lie down with your feet extended in front of you.
Let your arms relax by your side and the heels of your feet settle comfortably on the floor.

(2 seconds)

Gently close your eyes.
Allow your body to relax and get comfortable.

(5 seconds)

Now, bring your attention listen to any sound in the room.
Identify the various sounds in the room.

(5 seconds)

Now bring your attention back to your body. Let it relax, feel it soften and allow it settle down.

(10 seconds)

Begin to take some deep breaths that effortlessly flow in and out of your body.

(60 seconds)

Now, allow your breathing to take its normal breathing rhythm. Let go trying to control it.

(60 seconds)

Feel the sensations as the air goes in to your nostril, dropping behind your throat and finally filling your lungs.

(10 seconds)

Then as it leaves your lungs, passes behind your throat and out through the nostril.

(10 seconds)

Observe how effortless and seamlessly the air enters and leaves your body.

(30 seconds)

If your mind begins to wander, observe that it is wandering and bring back your attention to your breathing.

(10 seconds)

Continue to breath in and out without asserting any control.

(30 seconds)

Inhale and feel relaxation flow in your body. Exhale and release all the tension.

(10 seconds)

Breath in relaxation. Breathe out tension.

(10 seconds)

Become aware of your chest moving up and down with every cycle of breathing.

(20 seconds)

Notice how calm and relaxed your body is becoming.

(30 seconds)

Watch your breathing and be attentive to it.
If you notice that you are drifting off let my voice bring back your awareness to your breathing.

(30 seconds)

Breathe in relaxation. Breathe out tension.

(20 seconds)

Now, bring to mind the person that you want to let go. The person may still be in your life or not. They may have hurt you recently or in the past and you are no longer in contact with them.

(5 seconds)

Imagine him or her standing in front of you.

(5 seconds)

This person makes you feel negative emotions such as anger, resentment, bitterness and hurt, and you want to let go of the pain in your heart that they have caused you.

(5 seconds)

Direct your attention to your stomach and envision a silver cord that runs from your stomach to their stomach.

(10 seconds)

Feel it connecting the two of you.
Envision it pulsating as it gets energy from the connection.

(10 seconds)

Now, imagine that you are holding a pair of scissors in your hands.

(5 seconds)

Now take your hands towards the cord and notice as you cut through it. The cord may be tough and hard to cut but you gracefully keep cutting until you cut through.

(10 seconds)

Notice the cord break and separate.

(10 seconds)

Feel the connection between two of you dissolve. And, feel the freedom that accompanies your detachment.

(30 seconds)

Now, imagine a healing light surround the other person. Offer them your forgiveness, love, and blessings.

(10 seconds)

Watch as he or she slowly walks away from you.

(10 seconds)

You stomach now feels relaxed. The bitterness and resentment that was making it to become tensed is slowly dissolving.

(10 seconds)

You feel lighter, more peaceful and calm.

(10 seconds)

Now, pull the remaining energy cord to your stomach and seal it with a yellow light. Remind yourself that you have all your energy back with you and that you are safe.

(20 seconds)

Now scan your body for any signs of heaviness left behind.

(20 seconds)

Imagine yourself under a shower. Think of the water like a bright light and watch as it flows over your body. It is touching every part of your body from your head to your toes.

(20 seconds)

Let it cleanses your body of all the heaviness left behind.

(20 seconds)

Now, move your attention to your chest and imagine a green light in your heart center.

(5 seconds)

As you breathe in, the light expands and becomes bigger, as you breathe out the heart release all the tension. Keep breathing in and out gently as you allow the green light to dissolve all the tension and heaviness held in your heart.

(20 seconds)

Let the anger, bitterness and resentment go. Release all the anger and grief you feel. Let go of all the loss and self-loathing. Let whatever energy that is not serving you go. You deserve to be free of all the anger and resentment. You deserve to be at peace and to experience joy.

(30 seconds)

Continue to focus your attention to your heart. Allow the green light to become brighter and more vibrant.

(10 seconds)

Let the green light expand far above and around you forming an aura of protective and cleansing energy around you.

(10 seconds)

Now, bring to mind other people that may have hurt you either recently or a while back. Allow them a few inches into your aura of green energy. Look around and see each one of them. Remain Equanimeous and non-reactive as you look at each of them. Just become aware of their presence.

(20 seconds)

Now, repeat the following affirmations
I forgive you all that have hurt me.

(5 seconds)

I forgive myself for holding on to anger.

(5 seconds)
I let go all the anger, resentment, hurt and bitterness I feel.

(5 seconds)

I invite love and kindness into my life.

(5 seconds)

The aura of green light continues to expand around you as the people who hurt you walk away.

(10 seconds)

Now, visualize yourself living a peaceful and harmonious life. How do you feel? What does your everyday look like? How is your interaction with other people?

(20 seconds)

Let the green light return to your heart center. Remember it is always available for you whenever you need.

(5 seconds)

Become aware of your breathing. Notice your breath as it moves from your nostrils to your lungs.
Notice the air as it leaves your body and finds its way back to your immediate surrounding.

(20 seconds)

Continue to remain aware of your breath.

(120 seconds)

Gently wiggle your fingers and your toes. Move your head from side to side.

(10 seconds)

Become aware of the room you are in and the sounds in it.

(10 seconds)

When you are ready, open your eyes. Stretch your body a little bit and feel the new energy and bring it to the rest of your day.

Chapter 7: Self-love Meditation

Louise Hay in her book "You can heal your life" says that self-love is the solution to most of our problems. Many of us struggle with self-love. We are our biggest critics when indeed we should be our biggest cheerleaders. Self-love is not an "arrogant, know it all" attitude. Rather, it is a calm knowing, acceptance and approval of yourself.

How do you learn to love yourself? Begin with being kind to yourself and accepting yourself. Identify a person or a pet you love. How do you treat them, how do you handle them? and begin to practice that with yourself.

This guided meditation on self-love incorporates some affirmations on self-love. Repeat each affirmation at least three times before going on to the next.

While some people may fully resonate with the affirmations, it is possible that for some people saying these affirmations may bring up resistance. It might feel weird to say them. Say them anyway. If saying these affirmations brings up resistance, make a commitment to practice this meditation every day for the next 7 days. With time, the resistance will dissipate and you will begin to feel more in tune with yourself.

27.Guided meditation for self-love

Begin in an upright and seated position.
Take a deep breath in and a deep breath out.
Take two more deep breaths.

30 seconds

Now, notice your body in all its physicality. Your posture,
the different parts of your, and the various organs and
systems.
Notice how your body is functioning optimally to keep you
alive without your guidance.
It functions efficiently. The heart knows how to beat,
blood is flowing through your entire body, every organ is
carrying out it functions, the various organs and body
systems are working together efficiently.
Express gratitude for your body.

15 seconds

Notice the parts and aspects of body that you love.

30 seconds

Notice the parts of your body that you do not like then
affirm "I let go the self-hate I inflict on myself."

Repeat each affirmation three times

20 seconds
"I accept and love myself unconditionally".

20 seconds

 "I accept myself"

15 seconds

"I approve myself"

15 seconds

"I love myself"

15 seconds

"I am enough"

15 seconds

"I am worthy"

15 seconds

"I am good enough"

15 seconds

"I love and accept myself now"

15 seconds

"Every day I am learning to love myself"

10 seconds15 seconds

"I forgive myself for self-loathing and self-hating"

15 seconds

"I honor who I am"

15 seconds

"My being here matters"

15 seconds

"All is well in my life"

15 seconds

Take a few deep breaths.

30 seconds

Place your hands on your chest one at a time. Notice the warmth and positive energy you feel. Know that you are worthy, enough and that you matter.

28.Guided meditation for a positive self-image

Find a quiet place where you can sit or lie down comfortably.

(5 seconds)

Take three deep breaths and exhale completely.

(30 seconds)

Keep breathing deeply.

(30 seconds)

Now notice your hands – your fingers, the space between your fingers, nails and palms.

(10 seconds)

Notice your feet – your toes, the space between your toes, toe nails and the entire feet.

(10 seconds)

Visualize a relaxing light flowing from your head to your toes that washes away any tension and leaves you feeling relaxed.

(30 seconds)

Now, think about your perspective of yourself. How would you feel if had great self-esteem, confidence and self-acceptance?

(30 seconds)

A positive self-image is not perfection.

It is okay to have areas that need improvement.

It is alright to have things that you may want to change in yourself.

(10 seconds)

A positive or negative image is portrayed in self-talk.

When you make positive remarks about yourself, you maintain healthy self-esteem.

Contrary, if you make negative comments, you damage your self-esteem.

(10 seconds)

Positive thinking is portrayed in how you treat yourself.

Sometimes people change to be unique.

Sometimes they also change to be similar to others to avoid standing out.

There is nothing wrong with being different.

There is also nothing wrong with being similar to others.

(20 seconds)

Now, envision yourself having a jar of pure liquid relaxation. The liquid is in your favorite color.

(5 seconds)

Envision yourself having a soft paintbrush as well.

(5 seconds)

Visualize yourself opening the jar and dipping the brush in it.

When I mention a body part, envision yourself painting it slowly and notice as that part becomes relaxed.

Face

(5 seconds)

Neck and throat

(5 seconds)

Shoulders

(5 seconds)

Lower and upper back

(5 seconds)

Your right hand

(5 seconds)

Your left hand

(5 seconds)

Chest and stomach

(5 seconds)

Bottoms and hips

(5 seconds)

Your left thigh then the right thigh

(5 seconds)

Your left knee then the right knee

(5 seconds)

Right calf and left calf Calves

(5 seconds)

Left and right shin

(5 seconds)

Right foot ankles and left foot ankles

(5 seconds)

Left foot and right foot

(5 seconds)

Toes- all the ten toes

(5 seconds)

Notice how your body becomes relaxed from head to toes.

(5 seconds)

Become aware of any parts of the body that may need extra relaxation paint.

(5 seconds)

Pass some extra strokes of the relaxation paint on those parts.

(30 seconds)

Notice how much calmer your mind is.

(10 seconds)

Now, envision yourself with a positive self-image.

Imagine yourself as successful.

Imagine yourself as confident.

Imagine yourself as likable.

(20 seconds)

If you held yourself in high esteem, how would you show up in your everyday life.

(30 seconds)

What would you do differently?

(30 seconds)

Mistakes are a reminder that you are human. When you make mistakes, purpose to learn from them, and grow every day.

Offer yourself kindness and compassion when handling your mistakes, flaws and imperfections.

(20 seconds)

Let confidence, joy, and happiness grow inside you.

(20 seconds)

Now, I will count backward from three, and when I reach one, gently open your eyes.

Three

Two

One

Chapter 8: Chakra Healing Meditation

The term "chakra" is used in yoga, meditation and Ayurveda to refer to the main energy centers in the body. These chakras guided meditation will help you understand your energy system and heal any blockages to enable you function optimally mentally, spiritually, physically and energetically.

29. Beginner's Guided Chakra Awareness and Healing Meditation

Begin in a seated position. With your spine lengthened and legs crossed.

Become aware of what is happening around you.
What sounds do you hear?
What do you see?
What do you smell?
Can you sense the temperatures on your skin?

Now, take a deep breath and as you exhale gently close your eyes.
Turn your attention inwards. Notice your breathing.
Is it shallow or deep?

10 seconds

Notice a complete breath cycle as the air goes in and goes out.
And another breath cycle.

10 seconds

Notice the rise and fall of your chest when you breath.

10 seconds

Can you sense the air come in and go out of your nostrils?

10 seconds

Keep observing your breath and allow yourself to relax.

30 seconds

There are 7 chakras. Each is represented by a specific color, is located in a particular part of the body, and is responsible for particular emotions and physical aspects.

As I expound the various chakras, their roles and how they manifest, take your attention to the specific body part where the chakra is situated. From the information I provide about symptoms of blockages, reflect upon your emotions and observe your body to identify if you have symptoms of blockage at the specific chakra.

We will begin with the root chakra. It is located at the base of your spine. It is represented by color red and is responsible for giving you a sense of security, being grounded and safety.

An imbalance in the root chakra can manifest as anxiety and anxiety disorders, nightmares, being constantly worried even when it is not rational, and being fearful. Physically, you may experience back pain and issues with your bladder or passing stool.

The second chakra is the sacral chakra. It is located midway between your pubic bone and the navel. It is represented by color orange and is responsible for your creativity and sexual energy.

When balanced, you feel creative, free, abundant and joyous. On the contrary, when it is out of balance you may experience creativity blocks, depression, sexual dysfunction, a feeling of emotional instability, addiction, and anxiety towards change.

The third chakra is the solar plexus chakra, and is represented by color yellow. As the name suggests, it located at the solar plexus- a few inches above the navel at the meeting point of your ribs.

It influences your sense of identity, ambition, self esteem and a sense of personal power. It also supports digestion and metabolism.

When it is balanced, you feel self-confident, you have clear intentions and goals and the energy to move forward with them. Imbalances may manifest in form of low self-esteem, difficulty making decisions, anger issues, control issues and digestion problems.

The forth chakra is the heart chakra which is represented by color green. It is located at your chest center and influences your sense of social identity, love and relationships.

When it is open and balanced, you feel love, compassion, empathy and you forgive easily. When it is blocked, you keep grudges, feel jealous, angry and hatred towards yourself and others. You are also constantly in fear of betrayal. Heart chakra blockage may physically manifest as heart problems and respiratory problems or upper back pain.

The fifth chakra is the throat chakra which is depicted by color blue. It is located at your throat and influences your ability for self-expression, effective communication and integrity to speak your truth.

When open, you feel confident to express yourself. Otherwise, you may experience difficulty communicating, making decisions and you may experience mood swings. Physically, a blocked throat chakra may infest as stiff neck, sore throat, tooth aches, gum issues and thyroid problems.

The sixth chakra is the third eye chakra. It is situated between your eyebrows and is represented by color Indigo. It is influences your clarity of vision, intuition and ability for self-reflection.

If it is imbalanced, you may experience poor intuition, difficulty concentrating, depression, impaired judgment and confusion. Physically, a blocked third eye chakra may manifest as head aches, sleep problems, poor eyesight and nightmares.

The seventh chakra is the crown chakra. It is located at the top of your head and represented by color violet. It influences your self-knowledge, your spirituality and your connection to the divine.

Its imbalance may manifest in form of feeing lonely, lack of spiritual connection, and difficulty meditating. Physically you may experience migraines or tension headaches, sensitivity to light and sound as well as poor sleeping patterns.

Now that you have an understanding of the 7 chakras, let's go on to balance, open and heal each of them.

Take your attention to your root chakra.
Visualize a red circle of energy at the bottom of your spine. As you breath in, the red circle of energy intensifies and as you breath out, it cleanses all blocked energy and tension in this area.

Take five deep breaths.
With each inhale, the red circle of energy intensifies filling up every cell at the bottom of your spine and as you exhale it cleanses and melts away all the blocked energy in this area.

1 minute

Keep breathing and visualizing the red light.

10 seconds

Feel the surface beneath you and surrender the weight of your body to it. Relax your buttocks. Allow yourself to be supported and held steady by the surface beneath. You are safe, you are secure, you are grounded.
Let go your fears and your anxieties.

10 seconds

Repeat the following affirmations

"I am safe"
"I am divinely protected"
"All is well in my life"

"I am safe"
"I am divinely protected"
"All is well in my life"

"I am safe"
"I am divinely protected"
"All is well in my life"

Take a few more deep breaths here

30 seconds

Now, bring your attention to your Sacral Chakra. Imagine an orange light radiating at the space between your pubic bone and your navel.

As you breath in, the orange circle of energy intensifies and as you breath out, it cleanses all blocked energy and tension in this area.

Take five deep breaths.
With each inhale, the orange circle of energy intensifies filling up every cell between your pubic bone and your navel. As you exhale it cleanse and melts away all the blocked energy in this area.

1 minute

Keep breathing and visualizing this orange light.

10 seconds

Imagine yourself being creative, joyful and living an abundant life.
What activities do you see yourself engaging in?
How do you go about your everyday life?
See yourself as a creative being. Know that the information and ideas you need will come to you.

10 seconds

Repeat the following affirmations

"I am beautiful"
"I am creative"
"I am happy"

"I am beautiful"
"I am creative"
"I am happy"

"I am beautiful"
"I am creative"
"I am happy"

Take a few more deep breaths here

30 seconds

Now take your attention to your solar plexus. Imagine a yellow light radiating at the meeting point of your ribs.

As you breath in, the yellow circle of energy intensifies and as you breath out, it cleanses all blocked energy and tension in this area.

Take five deep breaths.
With each inhale, the yellow circle of energy intensifies filling up every cell between your navel and the meeting point of your ribs. As you exhale it cleanse and melts away all the blocked energy in this area.

1 minute

Keep breathing and visualizing the yellow light.

10 seconds

Become aware of your sense of self. Identify aspects of yourself that you love.
Your body, intelligence, talents, and skills.
Know that you are enough and you are worthy. See yourself as a confident person.
Own your personal power and your ambitions.

10 seconds

Repeat the following affirmations

"I completely love and accept myself"
"I am enough"
"I am worthy"
"I am empowered to live my best life"

"I completely love and accept myself"
"I am enough"
"I am worthy"
"I am empowered to live my best life"

"I completely love and accept myself"
"I am enough"
"I am worthy"
"I am empowered to live my best life"

Take a few more deep breaths here

30 seconds

Become aware of your heart chakra. Visualize a green light of energy radiating at your chest center.

As you breath in, the green circle of energy intensifies and as you breath out, it cleanses all blocked energy and tension in this area.

Take five deep breaths.
With each inhale, the green circle of energy intensifies filling up every cell around of the organs in your chest including the lungs, ribs and heart, and as you exhale it cleanse and melts away all the blocked energy in this area.

1 minute

Keep breathing as you visualize the green wave of energy.

10 seconds

Offer yourself love and compassion.
Forgive yourself for the times you were your own worst enemy.
Forgive people and situations that have hurt you.
Let it go. They do not serve you rather they take away from the fullness of your life.

10 seconds

Now, identify three people who you deeply love and send them loving and compassionate energy. Let your heart radiate loving energy.

10 seconds

Repeat the following affirmations

"I am willing to learn to love myself unconditionally"
"I forgive myself for inflicting self-hatred and criticism on myself"
"I am loving"
"I receive love effortlessly"
"I forgive and I am willing to let go all my past hurts and heartbreaks"

"I am willing to learn to love myself unconditionally"
"I forgive myself for inflicting self-hatred and criticism on myself"
"I am loving"
"I receive love effortlessly"
"I forgive and I am willing to let go all my past hurts and heartbreaks"

"I am willing to learn to love myself unconditionally"
"I forgive myself for inflicting self-hatred and criticism on myself"
"I am loving"
"I receive love effortlessly"
"I forgive and I am willing to let go all my past hurts and heartbreaks"

Take a few more deep breaths here

30 seconds

Now take your attention to your throat chakra. Visualize a blue light radiating on your throat area.

As you breath in, the blue circle of energy intensifies and as you breath out, it cleanses all blocked energy and tension in this area.

Take five deep breaths. With each inhale, the circle of energy intensifies filling up every cell around your throat and as you exhale it cleanses and melts away all the blocked energy in this area.

1 minute

Keep breathing and visualizing the blue light.

10 seconds

Identify some values and ideologies that you live by.

10 seconds

Identify situations in your life where you could have been more assertive and express of your truth but you did not.

10 seconds

Now visualize how you would have responded in these situations if you came from a place where you owned your self-power and you were able to communicate articulately.

10 seconds

Know that it is ok to be who you are and that it ok to be authentic.

10 seconds

Repeat the following affirmations

"I communicate effectively"
"I gracefully express myself"
"I own my truths"

"I communicate effectively"
"I gracefully express myself"
"I own my truths"

"I communicate effectively"
"I gracefully express myself"
"I own my truths"

Take a few more deep breaths here

30 seconds

Now take your attention to your third eye chakra.
Visualize an indigo light radiating at the space between your eyebrows.

As you breath in, the indigo circle of energy intensifies and as you breath out, it cleanses all blocked energy and tension in this area.

Take five deep breaths.
With each inhale, the indigo circle of energy intensifies filling up every cell around the space between your eyebrows and as you exhale it cleanse and melts away all the blocked energy in this area.

1 minute

Keep breathing and visualizing the indigo light.

10 seconds

Identify times in your life when you had a subtle nudge to take certain action or to make certain decision. When your intuition came calling but you ignored it.
What were the consequences?

10 seconds

Reflect on what your intuition felt like and commit to listen to it in future.

5 seconds

Identify some of your goals and intentions.
Pick one and visualize as much of it as possible.
 The steps involved, see yourself taking the steps, see the final outcome, and how it feels to achieve that goal.

15 seconds

Know that you have an inner guidance system that is always with you and that will help you achieve your goals and make the best decisions in life. Call upon your inner wisdom to help you to make good decisions, to see the big picture and to give you the grace to take the steps you need to achieve your goals and dreams.

10 seconds

Repeat the following affirmations:

"I trust my intuition"
"I acknowledge that I have inner wisdom and I am willing to listen to it"
"I am guided to make the best decision and take action for my highest good"

"I trust my intuition"
"I acknowledge that I have inner wisdom and I am willing to listen to it"
"I am guided to make the best decision and take action for my highest good"

"I trust my intuition"
"I acknowledge that I have inner wisdom and I am willing to listen to it"
"I am guided to make the best decision and take action for my highest good"

Take a few more deep breaths.

30 seconds

Take your attention to your crown chakra.

Visualize a purple light radiating at the top of your head. As you breath in, the purple circle of energy intensifies and as you breath out, it cleanses all blocked energy and tension in this area.

Take five deep breaths. With each inhale, the purple circle of energy intensifies filling up every cell in your head and as you exhale it cleanse and melts away all the blocked energy in this area.

1 minute

Keep breathing and visualizing this purple energy. Honor your spirit/soul and acknowledge your ability to connect with the divine.
Reflect upon what spiritual practices you have incorporated in your life. Meditation, prayer and self-reflection help to nurture your crown chakra. Commit to spend your time in one or more of these practices.

10 seconds

Repeat the following affirmations:

"I am connected to the divine within me."

"I am connected to the divine within me."

"I am connected to the divine within me."

Take a few more deep breaths.

30 seconds

Relax in this stillness. Allow your energy centers to rejuvenate and energize. Stay with the awareness of your 7 chakras. Take your attention from the root chakra, sacral chakra, solar plexus, heart chakra, throat chakra, third eye up to the crown chakra.

60 seconds

Know that you can trust the wisdom and intuition of your body.

30 seconds

Now come back to observing your breath. Notice it as it comes in and goes out through your nostrils. Effortless and rhythmic.

60 seconds

Take a deep breath in. Notice what is happening around your and when you are ready get on with the rest of your day.

30. Guided Chakra Meditation for Anxiety and Stress Relief

Find a comfortable position either seated or lying down and gently close your eyes.

(5 seconds)

Become aware of your surroundings. Are there any sounds in your immediate environment?

(5 seconds)

Is it warm or cold? Is the air humid?

(5 seconds)

The air you are breathing is it warm or cold? Does it have a smell or it is odorless?

(5 seconds)

Now, become aware of the parts of your body that are in contact with the ground. Allow your body to become limp and for the surface beneath you to support you.

(10 seconds)

Notice any sensations on your skin.

(10 seconds)

Notice any sensations on the different parts of your body.

(10 seconds)

Begin to take deep breaths.

(20 seconds)

Let the inhales and exhales allow you relax.

(20 seconds)

Notice as your chest rise and fall with every inhale and exhale.

(10 seconds)

Feel the sensation in your nostrils as you breathe in and out.

(10 seconds)

Become aware of the difference in temperature of the air that you are inhaling and the one that you are exhaling.

(20 seconds)
Now bring your attention to your tailbone, the bottom of your spine where the root chakra is located. Visualize a red circle of energy pulsating on the area around your tailbone. Take some deep breaths and visualize the energy going to your root chakra, easing any tension held on this part of your body

(30 seconds)

This root chakra is responsible for connecting you to the energy of the earth. When your root chakra is balanced, you feel grounded and supported. On the other hand, when your root chakra is overactive, you feel jittery and anxious. It might also manifest physically as digestive problems, lower back pain, hip pain, ovarian issues and prostate issues in men.

To balance your root chakra every day, incorporate grounding activities such as meditating and prayer in your everyday life. Also spend time in nature.

(10 seconds)

Repeat the following mantras to help you get grounded:

"I am here."

(5 seconds)

"I deserve to be here."

(5 seconds)

"The Earth is my support."

(5 seconds)

Take a few deep breaths here as you pay attention to the surface beneath you.

(30 seconds)

Now bring your attention to the area just below the belly button where your sacral chakra is located. Visualize an orange circle of energy pulsating around this area. Take some deep breaths and visualize the energy going to your sacral chakra, easing any tension held on this part of your body

(30 seconds)

This sacral chakra is responsible for your creative and sexual energy. When your sacral chakra is balanced, you feel motivated and relish in the joys of life without needing to over indulge. You are also sexually and creatively expressive. On the other hand, when your sacral chakra is overactive you have addictive and overindulgent tendencies. When it is underactive you experience a lack of passion, decreased sex drive and lack of creativity. Physically, it manifests as depression, obesity, hormonal imbalance and addiction.

To balance your sacral chakra, engage in creative activities often.
Repeat the following mantras,

"I am infinitely creative"

(5 seconds)

"It is ok for me to enjoy life"

(5 seconds)

"I let go the need to overindulge"

Take a few deep breaths as you pay attention to your sacral chakra.

(30 seconds)

Bring your attention the area on the top of your stomach where your ribs meet. This is where your solar plexus chakra is located. Visualize a yellow circle of energy pulsating around this area. Take some deep breaths and visualize the energy going to your solar plexus, easing any tension held on this part of your body

(30 seconds)

This solar plexus chakra is responsible for your sense of confidence and personal power. When your solar plexus chakra is balanced, you feel confident, a sense of wisdom, as sense of personal power and you are decisive. Otherwise, when it is underactive, you may feel timid, indecisive, insecure and needy. When it is overactive you may feel too energized, greedy, angry and have a need to control and micromanage.

Physically, in imbalanced solar plexus chakra manifests as digestive issues or issues on internal organs such as kidneys, liver, appendix and pancreas.

To balance your solar plexus chakra, recite self-esteem and self-confidence affirmations.

Repeat the following affirmation:

"I am enough"

(5 seconds)

"I am worthy"

(5 seconds)

"I am confident"

(5 seconds)

Take a few deep breaths here as you pay attention to the area around your solar plexus.

(30 seconds)

Now, move your attention to center of your chest where your heart chakra is located. Visualize a green circle of energy pulsating around this area. Take some deep breaths and visualize the energy pulsating in your chest area, easing any tension held on this part of your body

(30 seconds)

The heart chakra is responsible for your ability to give and receive love. It is also associated with compassion, kindness, empathy, joy and peace. of confidence and personal power. When your heart chakra is balanced you give and receive love with ease. You are kind and compassionate to others. When it is overactive, you may find it difficult to set healthy boundaries for yourself or you may experience interpersonal relationship issues. When it is underactive, you might find it difficult getting close to other people.

To balance your heart chakra, offer yourself self-love. Treat yourself with compassion and kindness and extend the same to other people. Engage in acts of service that are within your boundaries.

Repeat the following affirmation:

"I accept myself"

(5 seconds)

"I am willing to learn to love myself unconditionally"

(5 seconds)

"I am kind and compassionate to myself and others"

(5 seconds)

Take a few deep breaths here as you pay attention to the area around your heart center.

(30 seconds)

Now, move your attention to your throat where the throat chakra is located. Visualize a purple circle of energy pulsating around this area. Take some deep breaths and visualize the energy pulsating in your throat area, easing any tension held on this part of your body

(30 seconds)

The throat chakra is responsible for expressing your personal truth with clarity, love and kindness. If your throat chakra is overactive or interrupting others. When it is underactive, you may feel shy or opt to remain silent even on issues that are important to you. Physically, an imbalanced throat chakra may manifest as loss of voice, throat pain, cavities, or mouth ulcers.

When speaking always think:

"Is it the truth?"

"Is it necessary?"

"Is it kind?"

To balance your throat chakra practice expressing your emotions and truths.

Repeat the following affirmation:

"It is ok for me to speak my truth"

(5 seconds)

"Even when I feel like my truth does not matter, I will say it anyway"

(5 seconds)

"It is becoming easier and easier for me to speak my truth"

(5 seconds)

Take a few deep breaths here as you pay attention to the area around your collarbone and throat area.

(30 seconds)

Now, move your attention to the space between your eyebrows. This is where the third eye chakra is located. Visualize an indigo circle of energy pulsating around this area. Take some deep breaths and visualize the energy pulsating on the area around you're the space between your eyebrows, easing any tension held on this part of your body

(30 seconds)

The third eye chakra is responsible for intuition. It is believed to give the brain access to information that is beyond the material world and what your five senses can detect. When it is balanced you feel in tune with both yourself as well as the physical and material world.

You will receive intuitive messages with ease.
When it is overactive you may become obsessed with getting psychic information. On the other hand, when it is underactive, you may feel spiritually disconnected. Physically, an imbalanced third eye chakra may manifest as headaches, vision problems or sinuses.

To balance your third eye chakra, spend time in nature and engage in spiritual activities regularly.

Repeat the following affirmation:

"I am tuned in to my intuition"

(5 seconds)

"I am in alignment with the universe"

(5 seconds)

"I am divinely guided"

(5 seconds)

Take a few deep breaths here as you pay attention to the area between your eyebrows.

(30 seconds)

Now, move your attention to the top of your head where your crown chakra is located. Visualize a white circle of energy pulsating around this area. Take some deep breaths and visualize the energy pulsating on the area on the top your head, easing any tension held on this part of your body.

(30 seconds)

The crown chakra is responsible for pure conscious energy. It is the center of enlightenment and spiritual connection with your higher self. When it is balanced you feel in tune with your higher self and divine consciousness. When it is underactive, you may feel spiritually disconnected. Physically, an imbalanced third eye chakra may manifest as headaches.

To balance your crown chakra, engage in spiritual activities regularly and balance the other chakras.

Repeat the following affirmation:

"I am spiritual being experiencing humanness"

(5 seconds)

"I am connected to my highest self"

(5 seconds)

Take a few deep breaths here as you pay attention to the area around the crown of your head.

(30 seconds)

Once more visualize the various energy circles pulsating on all your chakras. A red circle of energy on your tailbone, orange circle of energy two inches below your belly button, a yellow circle of energy on your solar plexus, a green circle of energy on your chest, a purple circle of energy on your throat, an indigo circle of energy between your eyebrows and a white circle of energy on the crown of your head. See all the circles of energy vibrating simultaneously.
(30 seconds)

Now, bring your attention your body. Notice how your body feels and any sensations. Notice how calm, grounded and peaceful you feel and rest in this awareness.

(60 seconds)

Begin to deepen your breath.

(10 seconds)

Gently move your head from side to side.

(10 seconds)

Come to stillness and when you are ready gently open your eyes.

Chapter 9: Sleep Meditation

It is as important to end your day well as it you to start it. These evening guided meditations will help you recollect your energy, get calm and set you up for a good night's sleep. It is best to do them as the last thing before you sleep.

31.Guided Evening Meditation to unwind and prepare you for a good night's sleep.

Begin by setting up your space. Close the door, turn off your phone's notifications and put off or dim the lights.

When you are ready, settle down in a comfortable seated position either on your bed or on a chair.

Gently close your eyes.
Bring your awareness to your breath. Feel the rise and fall of your chest and belly.

20 seconds

Notice a breath cycle. A complete cycle as the air comes in and goes out.

Keep observing your breath cycles.

20 seconds

Allow yourself to let go and become relaxed with every breath.
Let you mind become quiet and your body still.

10 seconds

Pay attention to your inhale and exhale. Is your inhale longer than the exhale or is your exhale longer than the inhale? Just being aware and letting go any deliberate control of your breath.

20 seconds

Imagine, that with every inhale, a warm blue energy enters your body radiating healing and calming energy that enters every cell in your body.

And with every exhale, this blue wave of energy extends outside and forms an aura of calming and relaxing energy around you.

With every inhale, your body becomes calmer and with every exhale your aura widens.
You feel connected with yourself, the universe and life.

10 seconds

Now begin to reflect on the day that has been.

Reflect about all the things you are grateful for. The people you are grateful for in your life: your family, friends, colleges and the interactions you have had.

Express gratitude for the opportunities and insights that life presented to you today.

Express gratitude for both the small and big things in your life.

Notice how contented, joyous and good it feels to focus on gratitude.

10 seconds

Now, take a moment to let go the happenings of the day that weigh heavy on your heart. Any disappointments, frustrations, challenges, failures, and mistakes that you may have encountered today. Bring down the walls that may have built up around your heart today. Forgive yourself and anyone who may have wronged you.

Let it all go.

Take your attention to your heart. Allow it to open, to be tender and to be inhibited.
You did the best you could do today and that is enough. Let yourself off the hook on all the things you feel you should have done or could have done. Don't beat yourself up about anything.

Instead offer yourself compassion and say,
"I completely love and accept myself even with my imperfections."

Take a few deep breaths and let go any inhibitions you may be holding onto.

Now, take time to set your intentions for tomorrow. See yourself going through the day grounded, peaceful, contented and happy. Tomorrow presents another opportunity to live your life as best as you could. Purpose, to bring into your day a positive attitude. To enjoy the moments and to make the most out of them.

30 seconds

Now take your imagination to a time in the future. Where you are living your best life. You are incredibly happy. You love your life and yourself. Your life is purpose-filled. You know what you want out of this life and your inner guidance will help you figure it out. Surrender to the support of life and the universe.

30 seconds

Now, allow yourself a few moments of silence and stillness. Bring your attention to your body. Observe any sensations in your body. Observe your breath. Stay present and still.

3 minutes

Lie down and allow yourself to drift into sleep.

32. Guided imagery for sleep

Begin by setting up your sleeping area to make it conducive for a good night's sleep.
Close the main door, close the curtains, put on silent mode your social media accounts notifications, and switch off the lights and settle down in your bed.

Lay on your back, with your feet extended in front about hip-width apart or wider. Draw your covers up to your chest and rest your hands beside your body. Make any necessary adjustments to find a comfortable resting position.

Now, take a deep breath in and exhale completely emptying out your lungs.
Take another deep breath and allow the incoming fresh air to cleanse your entire body, bringing in a sense of relaxation.
As you exhale, let the outgoing breath take with it your cares and worries of the day.

Another day has come to the end. How do you feel about the day that has been? Take a few minutes to review your day.

...1 minute...
Notice what happened throughout your day from morning to evening. Without judgment, only pure awareness, notice the highs and lows of the day, the good and the not so good.

...1 minute...

Practice gratitude for the day that has been. People in your life, people you encountered, good health, being here, things and situations and anything else you feel grateful for.

...1 minute...

Now for a moment, give a bit of thought tomorrow.

...30 seconds...

What emotions come up when you think of the coming day?
Do you feel eager or anxious, energized or lethargic, worried?
Acknowledge how you feel without needing to fix it. Just being aware.
It is ok to feel what you feel.

...30 seconds...

Now, bring your attention back to the here and now.
Life is happening from moment to moment.
In each moment, you have the grace and strength to live it the best way that you can.
At this moment, allow yourself to surrender. Let go your worries and anticipations.

Take a deep breath in and breath out.
Inhale, exhale
Inhale deeply and completely exhale.
Keep breathing deeply

...1 minute...

Allow your body to release any tension it is holding to.
Allow your brain neurons to slow down and for your mind chatter to quieten.
Give yourself permission to relax and just be.

...30 seconds...

In this moment right here there no where to go, and nothing to do.
Just being here in now is enough. It is the highest appreciation of life.

...30 seconds...

Take a couple more relaxing deep breaths.

...1 minute...

I will lead you through a quick body scan to help your mind and body to relax even further.

Now, bring your attention to your feet.
Notice both big toes and the other toes on both feet.
Notice the soles of your feet, your heels and the tops of your feet.

Notice your ankles, your shins and your calves.

Take your attention to your knees, right thigh and then the left thigh.

Notice your pelvic area: the groin, hips and the buttocks.

Notice the lower back, the middle back, and the upper back.

Your belly, your ribs and your chest.

Take your attention to your fingers: the thumbs, index fingers, middle fingers, ring fingers and small fingers.

Notice the back side of your palms then the front side of your palms.

Take your attention to your wrists, forearms and elbows.

Shift your awareness to the biceps, triceps and shoulders.

The front and back of your neck.

From the back of the neck, draw your attention upwards to the entire skull.

Notice your forehead, the eyebrows, the space between your eyebrows, and your eyelids.
Notice your ears and nose, your cheeks and jaws, your upper lip and lower lip, and your teeth and tongue.

Now, randomly move your attention to the various parts of the body.

Your armpits, inner thighs and heels.

Notice your fingers, belly button and toes.

Now, the wrists, elbows and knees.

Keep moving your attention randomly across your body.

....1 minute...

You are relaxed, calm and present. lie down in this stillness as you observe your body

....1 minute...

Begin to deepen your breath.

....15 seconds...

Wiggle your fingers and toes Make circles with your wrists and ankles.
Straighten your hands past your head. Stretch like you are being puled on both sides.
Hug your knees to your chest tightly.
Roll over to your right hand side.
Stay here for a few seconds

....15 seconds...

Now, imagine a white light entering your body through your feet.
It penetrates the right sole of your foot.
It is calming and relaxing. It fills every cell in your right foot releasing any muscular tension. It continues to spread to your ankle, the entire left leg, into you knee and knee cap.
It flows slowly as it infiltrates every cell in your right leg, releasing muscular and any physiological stress stored in this part of the body.

...30 seconds...

The light proceeds to infiltrate every cell in your right thigh and glute. The tissues, blood vessels, muscles, tendons, and bone. It cleanses all the pent up stress.

...30 seconds...

Now, the light enters the left sole of your foot. It flows slowly and fills every cell in your right foot. It then spreads to your ankles, the entire left leg and the knee. Cleansing every cell, muscle and tissue.

...30 seconds...

It flows to your left thigh. Filling up every cell in your left thigh and leg buttock.

...30 seconds...

Both legs are filled with the warm, calming and relaxing white light. This light lingers here giving you a sense of calm and ease.

...30 seconds...

Now, the light spreads to the upper side of your body. Infiltrating your belly, ribs, chest, lower back, spine, mid back, upper back, all the organs and cells held in your torso, hands and neck. Releasing all tension held in this part of your body. The light lingers here giving you a sense of calm.

...30 seconds...

It then proceeds to your head. The scalp, crown of your head and the face. The entire face including your ears, eyes, cheeks, nose, lips mouth, forehead. Your face muscles relax and release the tension they are holding.

...30 seconds...

This light then deeply penetrates your brain. It creates a calming environment that helps your brain waves to transition from a beta sate to a relaxed alpha state. The light infiltrates your mind, illuminating all your limiting beliefs and negative thoughts that are making you tensed and anxious.

...30 seconds...

Now your entire body, every cell in your body is filled with this illuminating and calming light. From your head to your toes,

...30 seconds...

the front and back of your body.

...30 seconds...

From the skin, to the muscles to the bones.

...30 seconds...

As all the tension dissipates, the white light begins to expand outwards creating a aura of calm around you.

...30 seconds...

You lie down in stillness, calm and relaxation. It feels good to refresh your body and mind in this way.

....2 minutes...

Stay here with a calm awareness of our body.

Notice your breathing. As it comes in and goes out through your nose.
As it causes your chest to rise and fall.
As it causes your belly to rise and fall.

....2 minutes...

You may now roll over to your favorite sleeping position and allow yourself to rest.

33. Guided visualization to calm an overactive mind and for restful sleep

Lie down on a bed and adjust your body to a comfortable posture where you can safely fall asleep.

As your body and mind relax, you may fall asleep.

If you don't, it is still alright as your body and mind will be relaxed as well.

Begin to breath in deeply.
Exhale gently.

(5 seconds)

Inhale and exhale slow and calm breaths and allow your body to relax.

(20 seconds)

You don't have to do anything; just take slow and deep breaths.

(20 seconds)

Take a deep breath in and slowly release it, prolonging the exhale.

(10 seconds)

Take another breath in and then exhale slowly.

(10 seconds)

Continue breathing at this pace.

(30 seconds)

Now let your breath assume its own rhythm that is effortless and relaxing.

 (60 seconds)

Your body and mind are becoming more and more relaxed with each breath.

(30 seconds)

Notice your entire body supported by the surface beneath you.

Notice how still your feet are.

Feel them becoming heavy.

(10 seconds)

Imagine your feet getting warm.
Feel the warmth in your feet spreading up your legs.

(5 seconds)

Now, feel your arms becoming heavy and being supported by the surface underneath.
Imagine them sinking in the warmth of your beddings or on your cushions.

Notice as that warmth grows from your hands to the whole arm.

(20 seconds)

Feel the warmth from your legs, and the one from your arms make a connection in your stomach.

Notice your stomach becoming warm.
Notice the warmth spreading to your chest.

Feel the warmth overflowing to your back.
Notice how your back relaxes.

(20 seconds)

Your whole body feels heavy.
Your whole body is warm, and the bed feels cozier.
You feel an urge to cuddle your pillow, but your body is too heavy to move.

(10 seconds)

let your eyes sink heavily behind your eyelids.
They shut allowing you to lock out the external world and to rest.

(10 seconds)

Now, notice the sensations on your forehead.
Your forehead feels cool, calm, and relaxed.
There is no trace of tension on your forehead.

(10 seconds)

Envision tension escaping from your body through your toes and fingers.
Scan for any tension in your head- your eyes, ears, nose, ears, and cheeks.
Notice it flowing out of your body through the fingers.

(10 seconds)

Feel your head relaxing.

(10 seconds)

Become aware of your neck.
Scan for any tension in your neck.
Release it and watch as it flows out of your system through your fingers.

(10 seconds)

Observe your chest.
Can you feel any tension lodged there?
Release it and let it flow out of your body through the fingers.

(10 seconds)

Feel your stomach.
Check for any knots of tension in your stomach.
Visualize the tension going up to your shoulders
Down to your arms
And finally escaping through your fingertips.

(10 seconds)

Become aware of your back.
Check for any tension in the muscles in your back.
Scan for any tension lodged in your spine.

Release all that tension and feel it coming out through your fingers.

(10 seconds)

Listen to your upper body.
Notice how relaxed your upper body is.

(10 seconds)

Become aware of your hips and buttocks.
Check for any tension in your hips and buttocks.
Release the tension in that area.
Visualize as the tension flows down to your legs and comes out through your toes.

(10 seconds)

Feel your thighs.
Notice how strong they feel.
Feel the longest bone in your body- your thigh bone.
Check for any tension in your thigh bone.
Release all the tension in your thighs and feel then relax.

Notice the tension flowing down to your feet and leaving your body through the toes.
Feel your thighs becoming relaxed.

(20 seconds)

Move down further and become aware of your lower legs.
Notice your calves and your shins.
Feel all the muscles and veins in your lower leg.
Feel them tightening under tension.
Release all the tension in your lower legs and feel them becoming heavy.
Watch as the tension is washed out of the legs via the toes.
Feel your lower legs getting relaxed and calm.

(20 seconds)

Divert your attention to your ankles.
Do you feel any tension or pain in your ankles?
Release the tension lodged there and let it flow out through your toes.

(10 seconds)

Move your feet in a circular motion and check for any tension in your feet, soles, and toes.
Notice the areas that are tense and tired.
Release all the tension lodged there and feel your feet relaxing.
Visualize all the tension leaving hurriedly from your body through your toes and fingers.

With every breath you take, you can notice the tension draining away.
With every breath, you can feel the tension exiting through the fingers and toes.

(20 seconds)

Allow your mind to drift and relax.
You don't have to think or concentrate on anything.
Feel your body relaxing more as the tension drains away.
Feel it move through your veins to your fingers and toes.
Empty tension and replace it with relaxation in every part of your body.

(20 seconds)

Notice soft relaxation filling your body and mind.
Notice warm relaxation filling your body and mind.
Your body is becoming dense, and it is sinking deeper.
You are drifting to a pleasant sleep.

(30 seconds)

Gently, breathe in.
And breathe out.

(20 seconds)

Count one to ten

(10 seconds)
Now, I will begin to count backwards from 100. As I do so, concentrate on the numbers as I count them. (leave 3 seconds between numbers).

100 99 98 97 96 95 94 93 92 91 90 89 88 87 86
85 84 83 82 81 80 79 78 77 76 75 74 73 72
71 70 69 68 67 66 65 64 63 62 61 60 59 58 57
56 54 53 52 51 50 49 48 47 46 45 43 42 41 40 39 38
37...

Maintain your focus on the numbers and keep counting them.

(10 seconds)

Your mind and body are relaxed.

(10seconds)

Maybe you feel sleepy.

(20 seconds)

It is becoming difficult to concentrate on the numbers. Your mind wants to rest. Allow it to rest. Drift off to restfulness

(60 seconds)

You are drifting into a pleasant sleep.

With every breath you take, you are more relaxed.
With every breath you take, all you want to do is to sleep.

You are calm and sleepy.
You cannot count any longer.
It is alright; you can drift to sleep.

Surrender to your sleep.

(120 seconds)

Envision a beautiful place that is serene and calm.

Visualize your body floating in this beautiful place that is safe and serene.

(10 seconds)

Notice your body flying through the air gently.
This is the place is restful and peaceful.

 (10 seconds)

Slowly rest on the beautiful place and let your body sink in comfortably.
You do not need words to focus anymore.
Simply enjoy the feeling of relaxation.

(90 seconds)

Rest, Rest, Rest.

Chapter 10: Guided Meditation for Anxiety

Anxiety has become one of the leading mental issues globally. While there is a small percentage of the world population that struggles with clinical anxiety disorder, most of us struggle with every day anxiety. We are in the habit of constantly worrying which conditions our minds to operate in a low frequency constantly. While for some, it is mild, for others it can incapacitate their productivity, health and may lead to anxiety disorder.

Can you completely get rid of worry and anxiety? Not quite. But with a few tips and tools, you can be able to cope and live a more fulfilling life. Self-awareness plays a big role in detecting and managing anxiety. Meditation helps to cultivate this self-awareness, mental resilience and compassion for yourself. it also helps you to take a break from the racing, anxious thoughts and to reground yourself.

Theses guided meditations are one of the tools that you can add to your tool box to help cope with worry and anxiety. Either of the meditations will give you a break from the worrisome trail of thoughts and build your self-awareness and self-empathy. You can do it when you are feeling anxious or any time you need to feel calm and grounded.

34.Guided meditation to manage panic attack

This guided meditation is ideal for when you are experiencing a panic attack.

Become aware of your physical position at the moment. It doesn't matter if you are sitting, standing or lying down. Just become aware of the place your body is.

If you want to make some changes for better comfort, you may stretch and then sit down comfortably.

(10 seconds)

Right now, you may feel as if your life is in danger and it is okay to feel this way. This is how your body and mind is responding to this moment here and now. It is neither right nor wrong.

I know that you are feeling scared because of the panic attack but it will pass.

Do you feel as if you cannot breathe properly?

(5 seconds)

You may be breathing in a good amount of air but not breathing out enough.
The good news is that we can fix it now.

Part your lips slightly and slowly push air from your system through your lips as if you are whistling. Pay attention to how the air whizzes out of your lungs completely.

Now, take a deliberate deep breath in. Can you feel how the air fills your lungs back without any effort?

(10 seconds)

Breathe out again through your mouth slowly pushing the air out.

(5 seconds)

Keep taking deep breaths.

(30 seconds)

Keep inhaling deeply and slowly push the breath out through your mouth.

(30 seconds)

Now, allow your body to adapt to its natural rhythm of breathing.

(30 seconds)

In case you feel like your breathing is becoming strained again, become more deliberate about ensuring that you are exhaling completely.

(30 seconds)

You are safe and in no danger at all. Panic attacks are horrible and may make you feel physically uncomfortable but that is all there is.

You are in no danger.

(10 seconds)

Now bring your attention to your body. Feel as your shoulders drop to their natural position and the muscles around them become relaxed.

(10 seconds)

Are you clenching your jaw? Loosen your jaw abit and allow it to relax. Let your tongue rest between your lower set of teeth. Parts your lips slightly so that they are not too tightly closed against each other.

(10 seconds)

Notice how your heartrate. It is beginning to slow down. Soon, it will resume its normal rate.

(10 seconds)

Notice your breathing is becoming deeper, calmer and quieter.

(10 seconds)

Allow yourself to relax.

(10 seconds)

Listen to the following affirmations. They will help your thoughts to calm down.

I know that I am safe.

(3 seconds)

I have the ability to overcome panic attacks.

(3 seconds)

I am aware that these panic attacks cannot harm me.

(3 seconds)

I am okay and safe even though my heart is racing.

(3 seconds)

I am calm.

(3 seconds)

I can envision what relaxation feels like.

(3 seconds)

I can envision my whole body feeling centered and relaxed.

(3 seconds)

I am safe and calm.

(3 seconds)

I know that I am safe.

(3 seconds)

I have the ability to overcome panic attacks.

(3 seconds)

I am aware that these panic attacks cannot harm me.

(3 seconds)

I am okay and safe even though my heart is racing.

(3 seconds)

I am calm.

(3 seconds)

I can envision what relaxation feels like.

(3 seconds)

I can envision my whole body feeling centered and relaxed.

(3 seconds)

I am safe and calm.

(10 seconds)

Now, begin to count backwards from 100, 99,98,96....

(30 seconds)

In this moment, here and now, you are safe. Allow yourself to get calm.

(30 seconds)

Now pay attention to your breathing. Do not adjust your breathing but notice as you breathe in and as you exhale.

(10 seconds)

Start to count each complete breath. A complete breath is made up of one inhale and a subsequent exhale.

(20 seconds)

Keep counting your breaths and when you lose count, simply start from the beginning.

(30 seconds)

Continue to notice and count each breath.

(90 seconds)

You are now calm and relaxed.

(5 seconds)

You are now calm and relaxed.

(5 seconds)

You are now calm and relaxed.

(5 seconds)

Let your body and mind continue to relax and calm down.

(60 seconds)

When you feel ready, you can open your eyes and familiarize with your surroundings.

35. Guided Meditation to Instantly Relief Anxiety

Choose a comfortable seating position and sit with your spine straight and feet either on the ground or crossed.

Place your hands on your laps with the palms facing upwards.

(5 seconds)

Gently close your eyes.

(5 seconds)

Become aware of your whole body.

Take note of how your body feels from your head to your toes.

(20 seconds)

Inhale deeply and notice the air going through your nose to your diaphragm.

Hold it for a few seconds and then release the breath.

(5 seconds)

Continue breathing and notice your body relaxing every time you breathe out.

(10 seconds)

Inhale... exhale.

(10 seconds)

Become aware of any thoughts lingering in your mind.

Identify the dominant thoughts in your mind. What is it about?

Thinking is what the mind does. Do not get averse about the thoughts. Just observe them, like a curious onlooker.

(30 seconds)

Take note of the feeling or feelings associated with the dominant thoughts. Identify how those thoughts make you feel.

(30 seconds)

If the thoughts cause you gross sensations or emotions, focus on your breathing. Make your breathing deeper

(30 seconds)
When a positive thought pops in your mind, notice it as well and let it go without clinging to it.

(10 seconds)

You may find your mind wandering to the fears you have about life.
Do not be critical.
Notice it, but do not pursue it.
Notice the thought and let it go.

(30 seconds)

Envision yourself on a beach.
Imagine the sunrays diffusing in your skin.
Notice the breeze blowing your body, making you relax.

(5 seconds)

Visualize your thoughts as the wind.
Continue breathing and notice as the wind blows and stops.
Notice the wind sweeping past you as your thoughts keep changing.

(10 seconds)

Remain calm and keep breathing.

(20 seconds)

Remember that in this life, you are bound to experience anxiety.
You should never fight it.
Instead, welcome the feeling and notice as it is blown away by the wind.

(10 seconds)

When you experience happiness or joy remain aware of the pleasant emotions without clinging to them.

(20 seconds)

Begin to count from 10 to 1.

(20 seconds)

When you feel ready, become aware of the present moment.
Pay attention to your breathing.

(20 seconds)

Wiggle your toes and fingers.

(5 seconds)

Shake your hands and legs.

(5 seconds)

Move your head back and forth and the side to side.

(5 seconds)

Come back to stillness and gently open your eyes.

(5 seconds)

Reacquaint yourself with your immediate environment.
Look around and listen.
When you are ready, get on with the rest of your day.

Conclusion

Life is beautiful but also there are times when it is challenging and overwhelming.

The memories of the past can bring us much joy and nostalgia, yet they can be the one thing that holds us back from living fully now.

Likewise, the future can be a hopeful place we anxiously or excitedly look forward to, but today and now is all we are assured of.

Meditation reminds us to enjoy the now and make the most of it just as it is.
It may not make every moment perfect or take away all your problems, but it gives you a tool to enable you make the most of now. It can make each day a little better and at times "a little" better is enough.

It is a skill and the more you practice the better you become at it.

While there is scientific evidence to show that indeed meditation is a great tool for improving your quality of life, all the research and studies do not matter if meditation remains a concept in your life. Give it a fair chance in your life. Be patient with the process.

Remain consistent. Find a way to fit it in the most natural way to your lifestill.it will pay off.
I hope that this practice brings you a little bit calm, joy, centeredness, courage, hope, clarity and any other good in your life.

May you be happy,
May you be peaceful,
May you be harmonious.

Printed in Great Britain
by Amazon